Bible Brain Builders, Volume 2

Other Bible Brain Builders

Bible Brain Builders, Volume 1

Bible Brain Builders, Volume 3

Bible Brain Builders, Volume 4

Bible Brain Builders, Volume 5

Bible Brain Builders

Volume 2

THOMAS NELSON
Since 1798

NASHVILLE   DALLAS   MEXICO CITY   RIO DE JANEIRO

Published in Nashville, Tennessee, by Thomas Nelson. Thomas Nelson is a registered trademark of Thomas Nelson, Inc.

Book design and composition by Graphic World, Inc.

Original puzzles and mazes created by W. B. Freeman.

Thomas Nelson, Inc., titles may be purchased in bulk for educational, business, fund-raising, or sales promotional use. For information, please e-mail SpecialMarkets@ThomasNelson.com.

ISBN: 978-1-4185-4913-8

Printed in Mexico

14 13 12 11 QG 1 2 3 4 5 6

Songs of Joy

*T*he angels were the first to sing at Christmastime as they announced the birth of the Savior praising God saying, "Glory to God in the highest, and on earth peace, goodwill toward men." The singing of carols has become a favorite custom worldwide, proclaiming the glad tidings of the Christmas message.

The word *carol* comes from a word that meant a dance performed in a circle. It is thought that originally the dance was accompanied by flute music and eventually by singing. Carols were sung between acts of the mystery plays that told the stories of the gospel before the Bible was widely available to the general public. Through the years, carols were sung and performed at different seasons and holidays but are now associated primarily with Christmas.

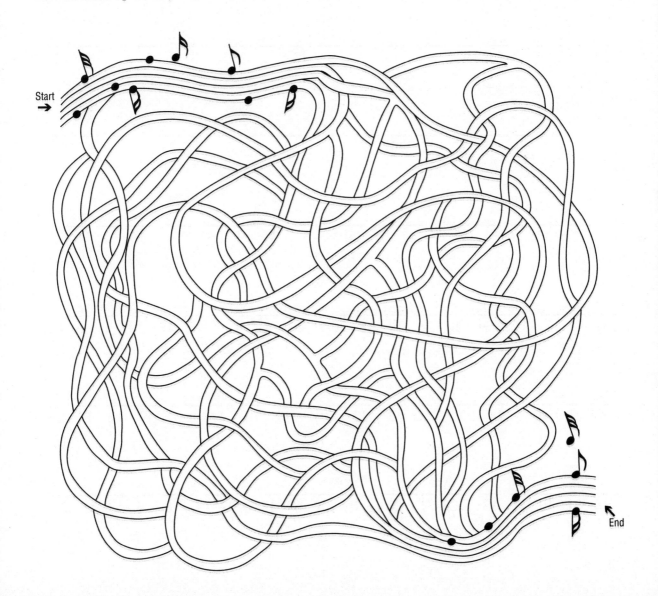

What is the Lord's due and why? Solve this cryptogram to discover a Bible answer.

Clue: MESSIAH *is* 2 18 11 11 10 26 12

—— —— —— —— —— —— —— —— —— —— —— ——' —— —— —— —— ——'
23 3 15   26 9 18   19 3 9 13 12 23   3   4 3 9 20

—— —— —— —— —— —— —— —— —— —— —— —— —— —— —— —— —— ——
13 3   9 18 22 18 10 17 18   14 4 3 9 23   26 1 20

—— —— —— —— —— —— —— —— —— —— —— —— ——; —— —— ——
12 3 1 3 9   26 1 20   5 3 19 18 9   16 3 9

—— —— —— —— —— —— —— —— —— —— —— —— —— —— —— —— —— —— ——
23 3 15   22 9 18 26 13 18 20   26 4 4   13 12 10 1 14 11

—— —— —— —— —— —— —— —— —— —— —— —— —— —— —— —— —— ——
26 1 20   24 23   23 3 15 9   19 10 4 4   13 12 18 23

—— —— —— —— —— —— —— —— —— —— —— —— —— —— —— —— —— —— ——.
18 21 10 11 13   26 1 20   19 18 9 18   22 9 18 26 13 18 20

Unscramble the letters in Column B to find the names of the brothers and sisters of the person(s) in Column A. When you finish with this acrostic you will discover a word that describes how Christians, as brothers and sisters in the Lord, are related to one another.

Column A

1. JAMES (Matthew 4:21)
2. TAMAR (2 Samuel 13:1)
3. JACOB (Genesis 25:26)
4. AARON, MIRIAM (1 Chronicles 6:3)
5. JOSEPH (Genesis 35:24)
6. ABEL, CAIN (Genesis 4:25)
7. MAHLON (Ruth 1:2)
8. MARY, MARTHA (John 11:1–3)
9. SIMEON, LEVI (Genesis 34:25)
10. PHINEHAS (1 Samuel 4:4)
11. ALEXANDER (Mark 15:21)
12. KOHATH, MERARI (Genesis 46:11)
13. ASAHEL, ABISHAI (2 Samuel 2:18)
14. ELIAB, DAVID, SHAMMAH (1 Samuel 17:13–14)

Column B

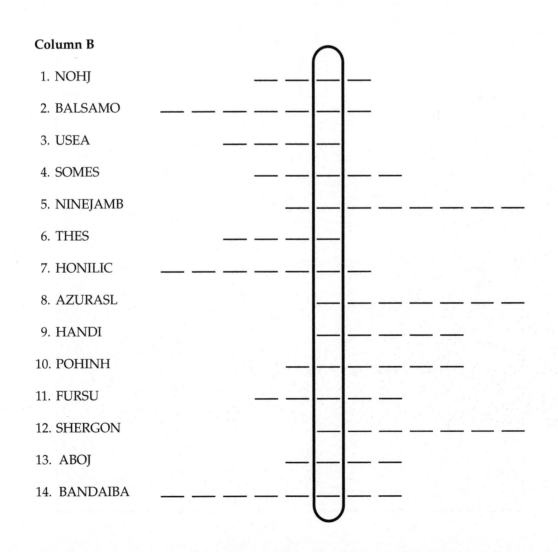

1. NOHJ
2. BALSAMO
3. USEA
4. SOMES
5. NINEJAMB
6. THES
7. HONILIC
8. AZURASL
9. HANDI
10. POHINH
11. FURSU
12. SHERGON
13. ABOJ
14. BANDAIBA

MOSES THE MEDIATOR

Moses met with God on the mountaintop and received a code of law for the people of Israel and the great promises of God to be with His chosen people. But before he left the mountaintop, Moses was warned of trouble ahead.

While Moses was away, the shortsighted Israelites grew impatient and lost hope. And so they made for themselves another god — an idol, a calf of gold — and danced around it.

When Moses got down from the mountain and saw these rebellious people, his "anger became hot," and he smashed the stone tablets of God's Law into pieces. He announced he would go back to the Lord: "Perhaps I can make atonement for your sin."

Moses asked God to forgive their sins. But sin could not be overlooked, and God said those who sinned would be blotted out of His book. He also told Moses that He would send His angel before them to the promised land but that His presence would not go with them. The people mourned when they heard this bad news. So Moses met again with God on behalf of the people, "If Your Presence does not go with us, do not bring us up from here."

God listened to Moses, and Moses found grace in God's sight. And because he did, God renewed His covenant with the people saying, "Before all your people I will do marvels such as have not been done in all the earth. . . . It is an awesome thing that I will do with you."

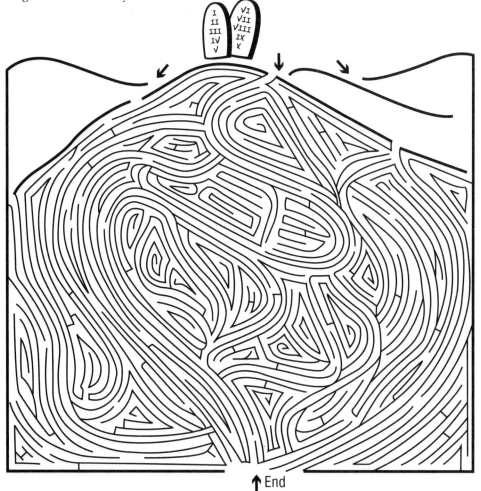

↑ End

Pursued!

When Saul heard the women sing, "Saul has slain his thousands, and David his ten thousands," it put him over the edge. For him it was the ultimate put-down; his very reputation as king had been based on his great success as a warrior and military commander. But the Scripture says, "Saul was very angry, and the saying displeased him. . . . So Saul eyed David from that day forward" (1 Samuel 18:8–9).

Saul's obsessive jealousy over David consumed his final years as Israel's king. One day when David was playing music to calm Saul's madness, Saul came to him with a javelin. Saul led his best men in pursuit of David as he hid in the wilderness from the enraged king. All this happened in spite of David's expressed and real loyalty to King Saul.

Saul's last days were tragic. The army of Israel fell against the enemy Philistines. And when the Philistines pursued Saul and his sons, they killed Jonathan, Abinadab, and Malchishua and wounded Saul. The fallen king then took his own life rather than risk abuse at the hands of his enemies.

Help David escape without being captured by Saul's army. Note: King Saul and his soldiers are looking for David in all four directions.

NEHEMIAH'S LATE-NIGHT RIDE

After Nehemiah returned to Jerusalem and had been in the city three days, he got up in the night and, taking only a few men with him, rode around the city of Jerusalem. He thoroughly surveyed the broken-down walls, the burned-out gates, and the rubble of the city. The Bible says that none of the officials of the city knew where Nehemiah had gone or what he had done. Nehemiah had not yet told the Jews, the priests, the nobles, the officials, or the workers about his plan to rebuild the city. (See Nehemiah 2:11-16.)

The project of reconstructing the city's walls took fifty-two days to complete under Nehemiah's skillful and courageous leadership (Nehemiah 6:15). When the Israelites' enemies heard of it, they were disheartened because they knew such a great task could only be accomplished with God's help on the Israelites' behalf.

Help Nehemiah find his way all around Jerusalem without being spotted by anyone who may be looking out the windows labeled *W*.

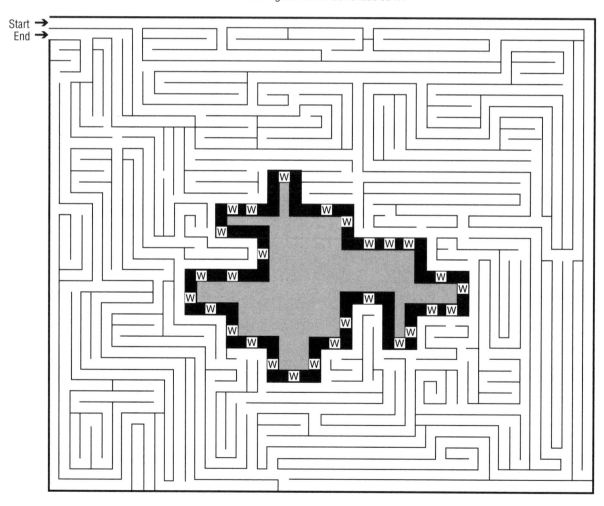

*F*ind the names of the seven who were appointed to "serve tables".

E	S	N	S	P	H	I	L	P	A
M	S	A	A	R	P	E	T	S	P
A	P	N	L	N	P	H	E	A	R
C	S	T	E	O	N	E	R	N	O
I	T	E	L	I	C	M	T	I	C
N	E	O	C	O	E	I	S	C	H
S	P	A	S	N	S	P	N	A	O
O	H	H	A	R	N	A	T	P	R
N	E	S	I	T	O	C	E	R	U
P	N	M	I	L	M	I	P	O	S
R	O	N	A	C	I	N	N	M	E
E	T	S	M	I	T	P	S	A	N

Rulers – yet still subject to the Lord God, King of the universe!

Across

1 He ordered the priests to receive offerings to repair the temple

8 He is described as the king "who sinned and who made Israel sin"

9 His evil wife was Jezebel

10 The Lord was pleased with his request for an "understanding heart"

12 He burned the king's house down around himself and died in the fire

14 Jeroboam's son, he ruled Israel only two years

15 He was only 8 years old when he became king, and he did "what was right in the sight of the LORD"

17 Jeroboam's son, he reigned over Israel in Samaria only 6 months

18 He gave the king of Assyria 1,000 talents of silver to buy peace

20 King of Judah, he made peace with the king of Israel

21 Son of Ahab, he worshiped Baal and provoked the Lord God of Israel to anger

23 He reigned only a month in Samaria before he was killed

25 He became a leper and lived in an isolated house

28 He "did not leave to Jeroboam anyone that breathed until he had destroyed him"

30 The king of Egypt deposed him after he ruled only 3 months

31 He was killed in the citadel of the king's house

32 Ahab's son; he did evil in the Lord's sight

Down

1 He became king at age 18 and reigned 3 months before king Nebuchadnezzar took him to Babylon

2 Israel's first king

3 Son of Solomon, he reigned in Judah

4 He bought the hill of Samaria during his 12-year reign as king of Israel

5 He reigned in Hebron over Judah for 7-1/2 years and in Jerusalem over Israel and Judah for 33 years

6 Even though his heart was not loyal to God, the Lord "gave him a lamp in Jerusalem" for the sake of his father David

7 Best known for building the Upper Gate of the Lord's house

11 He sent the silver and gold from the Lord's house to enlist the military aid of the king of Assyria

13 He shed innocent blood "till he had filled Jerusalem from one end to another"

16 He "trusted in the Lord God of Israel, so that after him was none like him among all the kings of Judah"

19 He killed 10,000 Edomites in the Valley of Salt

22 King of Judah, he warred against Baasha, king of Israel,"all their days"

24 He built Elath and restored it to Judah

26 He "sacrificed to all the carved images which his father Manasseh had made, and served them"

27 Jehu conspired against him

29 He wrote a series of letters to Ahab's 70 sons in Samaria

Word Pool

ABIJAM AHAB AHAZ AHAZIAH AMAZIAH AMON ASA AZARIAH
BAASHA DAVID HEZEKIAH JEHOAHAZ JEHOASH JEHOIACHIN JEHORAM
JEHOSHAPHAT JEHU JEROBOAM JORAM JOSIAH JOTHAM MANASSEH
MENAHEM NADAB OMRI PEKAHIAH REHOBOAM SAUL SHALLUM SOLOMON
UZZIAH ZECHARIAH ZIMRI

RESURRECTED!

The butterfly is not mentioned in Scripture, but it has become a popular symbol of the new life in Christ and the resurrection. Metamorphosis, the life cycle of the butterfly from the egg to the larva, the pupa, and finally the beautiful adult butterfly, symbolizes the conversion of the Christian as he or she becomes increasingly Christlike, conformed to the image of Jesus. The butterfly emerges from its cocoon with a "glorified" body to soar to heights impossible to the insect in its life as a caterpillar.

Start

End

By adding and subtracting the numbers in this puzzle, you will find the difference in the number of books in the Old and New Testaments.

The number or books in the Old Testament _____

Plus …
The number of books in the Pentateuch   + _____

Plus …
The number of books of Old Testament history   + _____

Minus …
The number of epistles in the New Testament   − _____

Minus …
The number of books of Old Testament prophets   − _____

Plus …
The number of books in the Old Testament of
poetry and wisdom   + _____

Plus …
The number of gospels about the life and
ministry of Jesus   + _____

Equals …
The number of books in the New Testament   = _____

*H*ere you'll find the tall and the short!

Across

2 Giants were thought to be the
____ of the sons of God and
the daughters of men

4 Tall tower name ____
"because there the LORD
confused the language of all
the earth"

6 The spies "____ our hearts" by
telling of a people greater and
taller in the promised land

10 "There were giants on the
____ in those days…. Those
were the mighty men who
were of old"

12 The Israelites felt like this in
comparison to Anak's descendants

15 Giant slain by David

16 Goliath was called a "____" of
the Philistines

17 One of Goliath's brothers

22 Known as giants, they lived in a valley (see #20 Down)

23 Name given to the city formerly known as Kirjath Arba, the name of a giant

24 From his shoulders upward he was "taller than any of the people"

25 Greatest man among the Anakim

Down

1 Name for the region "at the top of the skies"—the place where the Tower of Babel reached

2 "I will cut down its tall ____ and its choice cypress trees"

3 Jacob dreamed of one so tall that its top reached into heaven

5 The Moabite name for the tall people in the land of Ar

7 King of Bashan, his bed was 9 cubits long

8 A giant who lived in this place had 24 fingers and toes

9 Son of a giant

11 With Argob, all of this region was called "the land of the giants"

13 The staff of Goliath's was like a weaver's beam

14 Bible people noted for their great height

15 The Anakim and Emim peoples

18 The giants were called the "____ men who were of old"

19 King was taller than any of his people "from the shoulders ____"

20 The ____ of Rephaim may be translated "Valley of the Giants"

21 The people of Babel built a ____ "whose top is in the heavens"

Word Pool

ANAKIM ARBA BABEL BASHAN CEDARS CHAMPION CHILDREN DISCOURAGED
EARTH EMIM GATH GIANTS GOLIATH GRASSHOPPERS HEAVENS HEBRON
LADDER LAHMI MIGHTY OG REPHAIM SAUL SPEAR SIPPAI TOWER
UPWARD VALLEY

*S*tring together the words to reveal a famous choice. What will YOUR choice be?

C	H	V	E	S	T	Y	W	W	U
S	O	L	S	H	I	A	H	I	O
O	E	E	R	S	D	O	M	Y	L
W	I	F	U	O	V	R	E	S	L
E	L	L	O	Y	B	E	A	S	O
W	S	T	H	R	U	T	M	R	F
E	E	E	E	L	H	Y	M	E	A
R	V	S	U	O	O	R	D	D	N

It was more than just a dream; it was prophecy. Unscramble the words on the left and match them with their correct description on the right.

1. ASRMEOPG

___ ___ ___ ___ ___ ___ ___ ___

A. And he who overcomes, . . . to him I will give power over the nations.

2. RSSDIA

___ ___ ___ ___ ___ ___

B. Be faithful until death.

3. SEHSUPE

___ ___ ___ ___ ___ ___

C. Be watchful, and strengthen the things which remain.

4. DAELIACO

___ ___ ___ ___ ___ ___ ___ ___

D. I will make those of the synagogue of Satan, . . . come and worship before your feet.

5. RATHITAY

___ ___ ___ ___ ___ ___ ___ ___

E. You have there those who hold the doctrine of Balaam.

6. LAHIDPIHEPLA

___ ___ ___ ___ ___ ___ ___ ___ ___ ___ ___

F. I counsel you to buy from Me gold refined in the fire.

7. YASMNR

___ ___ ___ ___ ___ ___

G. Remember . . . from where you have fallen.

Match

1 - ___

2 - ___

3 - ___

4 - ___

5 - ___

6 - ___

7 - ___

14

There are many instances in the Bible of God's revealing His plans and speaking to people in their dreams. Fill in the answers below with answers that relate to dreams in the Bible.

Across

1. In matters of wisdom and understanding, Daniel and his three friends were ten times better than____(Daniel 1:20)
4. In his dream, eleven ____ bowed to Joseph (Genesis 37:9)
7. "____for you, O king, thoughts came to your mind while on your bed" (Daniel 2:29)
9. King Nebuchadnezzar was____ by his dreams (Daniel 2:1)
13. In Jacob's dream, this device stretched to the heaven (Genesis 28:12)
14. Solomon asked to be able to discern between good and____ when God asked him in a dream what he wanted (1 Kings 3:9)
15. Joseph interpreted the baker's dream that he would hang from a ____ (Genesis 40:19)
16. Solomon explained to the Lord that he was a "little child; I do not know how to go____or come in" (1 Kings 3:7)
17. This man was released from prison to interpret a dream for Pharaoh (Genesis 41:14)
20. Evening (old English)
21. Jacob lifted his____"and saw in a dream" (Genesis 31:10)

22 God____(past tense) Pharaoh in his dreams "what He is about to do" (Genesis 41:25)

24 This Babylonian king could not sleep because of his dreams (Daniel 2:1)

27 God revealed to Abimelech in a dream that____was Abraham's wife (Genesis 20:3)

29 When he told his brothers his dreams, Joseph ended up in this far country (Genesis 37:28)

30 This ruler had dreams about the years of plenty and famine that would come to his nation (Genesis 41:25)

32 To awaken;____up

34 When Jacob awoke, he said, "Surely the LORD is in this____" (Genesis 28:16)

35 Images or a message occurring during sleep: God sometimes communicates in this way

38 Joseph was told in a dream that Mary's son would save people from their____(Matthew 1:21)

40 In a dream, God told Jacob "the ____on which you lie I will give to you and your descendants" (Genesis 28:13)

41 Joseph asked, "Do not interpretations belong to ____?" (Genesis 40:8)

42 This man remembered Joseph's interpretation of his dream and introduced him to Pharaoh (Genesis 41:9–12)

44 The angel told Joseph in a dream, "Do not be____" (Matthew 1:20)

45 The butler dreamed that the vine brought forth this fruit (Genesis 40:10)

46 In Jacob's dream, the____of God were ascending and descending the ladder

49 Opposite of #16 Across

51 The top of #13 Across reached to ____(Genesis 28:12)

52 On the third____,which was Pharaoh's birthday, the baker and butler were released from prison (Genesis 40:20)

53 These animals, fat and gaunt, represented years of abundance and famine in Pharaoh's dream (Genesis 41:26–27)

54 The angel let Joseph know in a dream that Mary was the fulfillment of the prophecy "Behold, the virgin shall____ with child" (Matthew 1:23)

55 In Joseph's dream, eleven of these bowed to Joseph's____ (Genesis 37:7)

56 The number of good heads of grain in Pharaoh's dream (Genesis 41:5)

57 The feet and toes of clay and iron in Nebuchadnezzar's dream indicated the kingdom will be ____(Daniel 2:41)

Down

1 God spoke to this king of Gerar in a dream (Genesis 20:2–3)

2 The Angel of God told Jacob in a dream, to look at this animal (Genesis 31:12)

3 In a dream, God told #23 Down to speak neither____nor bad to Jacob (Genesis 31:24)

5 The butler and baker were ____ when Joseph came in to them (Genesis 40:6)

6 The sheaves and stars____to Joseph in his dreams (Genesis 37:7, 9)

8 In his dream, this man was reassured of God's covenant with him and his people (Genesis 28:13–15)

9 In the butler's dream, the ____ branches were ____ days (Genesis 40:12)

10 Joseph's____hated him when he told them his dreams (Genesis 37:8)

11 Joseph told the baker, "The birds will____your flesh from you," (Genesis 40:19)

12 The Lord appeared to Solomon in a dream at____(1 Kings 3:5)

18 She, opposite

19 "He, who ____s secrets has made known to you what will be" (Daniel 2:29)

23 Jacob's father-in-law (Genesis 31:24)

25 Formerly Luz: where God spoke to Jacob in a dream (Genesis 28:19)

26 The butler dreamed that he pressed the grapes into Pharaoh's____(Genesis 40:11)

28 God told Solomon in a dream, "____! What shall I give you?" (1 Kings 3:5)

31 Solomon asked for an understanding____(1 Kings 3:9)

33 The king commanded that all the ____men of Babylon be killed (Daniel 2:12)

34 Jacob made a____out of the #47 Down he had slept on and poured oil on it (Genesis 28:18)

35 "God has shown Pharaoh what He is about to ____" (Genesis 41:25)

36 Joseph did as the angel____ and took to him Mary as his wife (Matthew 1:24)

37 "There is a God in heaven who reveals ____" (Daniel 2:28)

39 Daniel asked the king for time that he might be able to____ the king's dream (Daniel 2:16)

42 This man's dream foresaw his demise (Genesis 40:22)

43 Solomon asked God for the ability to____between good and evil (1 Kings 3:9)

47 The____that Jacob had used for a pillow, became #34 Down (Genesis 28:18)

48 Joseph told the Pharaoh, "It is not in____; God will give Pharaoh an answer" (Genesis 41:16)

50 God told #1 Down in a dream that he had taken another man's ____(Genesis 20:3–8)

51 In a dream Joseph was told to "take the young Child and____ mother, flee to Egypt" (Matthew 2:13)

55 God gave Solomon wisdom, riches, and honor "____that there shall not be anyone like you among the kings all your days" (1 Kings 3:12–13)

This cryptogram is part of a sermon.

Clue: MESSIAH is CHNNKUJ

R B H N N H S   U W H

Q J H   E Z Z W   K D

N E K W K Q '   Y Z W

Q J H K W N   K N   Q J H

I K D F S Z C   Z Y

J H U M H D.

The earth provides food and shelter for God's creatures. Hidden in the letter box below are the names of some of God's creatures, and the food and the habitation that He provides for them. All the words are found in Psalm 104:10–26.

```
S  Y  E  K  N  O  D  P  O  N  S  S  T  O  R  K
X  F  O  P  O  R  S  M  A  N  T  P  L  X  N  Q
A  S  F  I  T  A  Q  W  G  N  X  R  U  O  L  U
Z  V  L  I  V  E  G  E  T  A  T  I  O  N  I  Q
L  Z  A  B  L  Q  B  A  N  D  O  N  R  S  O  B
E  A  T  T  I  C  E  O  Y  G  S  G  N  O  N  S
O  A  T  R  U  E  A  Q  T  R  U  S  T  A  S  M
B  A  D  G  E  R  S  T  A  O  G  X  H  P  O  T
C  O  A  W  E  R  T  S  E  E  R  T  P  O  X  N
I  C  E  O  I  S  P  O  X  N  A  L  I  E  P  O
S  S  R  A  D  E  C  Z  B  I  S  O  W  N  P  Q
A  B  B  O  D  A  O  N  V  A  S  L  L  I  H  Z
P  B  I  R  D  S  N  E  O  Z  L  G  P  W  J  N
P  O  N  Q  G  X  L  P  N  Q  U  T  R  I  F  N
```

Word Pool

BADGERS BEAST BIRDS BREAD CATTLE CEDARS CLIFFS DONKEYS
FIR GOATS GRASS HILLS LEVIATHAN LIONS MAN
OIL SEA SPRINGS STORK TREES VEGETATION WINE

*I*t was King David's desire to build a permanent temple for the Lord that would be the center of worship for the children of Israel. But because David was a man of war God did not allow him to build the temple. Instead God told David that his son, Solomon, would build it. The details of the temple "blueprints" are spelled out in 1 Kings 6. Fill in the correct numbers in this puzzle, perform the math functions and you will arrive at the number of years it took to build the temple. All of the measurements are in cubits.

The length of the temple   _____

Multiplied by …
The height of the side chambers   ×   _____

Plus …
The length in front of the temple sanctuary   +   _____

Divided by …
The number of cherubim in the inner sanctuary   ÷   _____

Plus …
The height of the temple   +   _____

Divided by …
The width of the temple   ÷   _____

Plus …
The length of each wing of the cherub   +   _____

Plus …
The length of the vestibule in front of the sanctuary   +   _____

Divided by …
The width of the lowest chamber   ÷   _____

Equals …
The number of years it took to build the temple   =   _____

LIGHT IN THE DARKNESS

*I*n the Scripture the lamp symbolizes guidance and wisdom, giving divine light and understanding. The Bible describes the Word of God as a lamp unto our feet and a light to our path (Psalm 119:105). "For the commandment is a lamp, and the law a light" (Proverbs 6:23). Scripture also describes the Lord as our lamp, the One who lightens our way: "For You are my lamp, O Lord; the Lord shall enlighten my darkness" (2 Samuel 22:29).

Jesus used the metaphor of the lamp to teach believers about their responsibility to those in darkness. In the Sermon on the Mount, Christians are told to set their lamp on a lampstand so that it will give light to "all who are in the house" (Matthew 5:15). Christians are to allow the light of Christ in their lives and their good works to give light to those in darkness.

In the parable of the ten virgins, Jesus taught that Christians are also responsible to keep an adequate supply of oil in their "lamps" so they are not without light. It was the wise virgins who kept enough oil in their lamps to keep them burning until the bridegroom came.

*I*n Genesis 46, we are told about Jacob's family members as they left for Egypt. Below is Jacob's family tree. Your challenge is to put the names in the grid provided on the opposite page. We've given you some letters as a starting point. Unscramble those letters to learn something about these people.

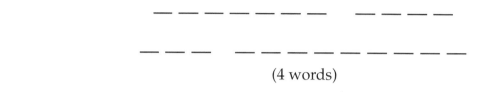

(4 words)

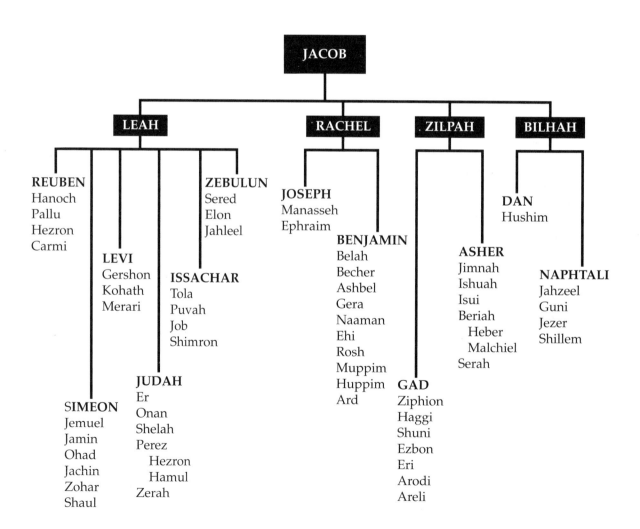

JACOB

LEAH **RACHEL** **ZILPAH** **BILHAH**

REUBEN
Hanoch
Pallu
Hezron
Carmi

ZEBULUN
Sered
Elon
Jahleel

JOSEPH
Manasseh
Ephraim

DAN
Hushim

LEVI
Gershon
Kohath
Merari

ISSACHAR
Tola
Puvah
Job
Shimron

BENJAMIN
Belah
Becher
Ashbel
Gera
Naaman
Ehi
Rosh
Muppim
Huppim
Ard

ASHER
Jimnah
Ishuah
Isui
Beriah
  Heber
  Malchiel
Serah

NAPHTALI
Jahzeel
Guni
Jezer
Shillem

JUDAH
Er
Onan
Shelah
Perez
  Hezron
  Hamul
Zerah

GAD
Ziphion
Haggi
Shuni
Ezbon
Eri
Arodi
Areli

SIMEON
Jemuel
Jamin
Ohad
Jachin
Zohar
Shaul

19

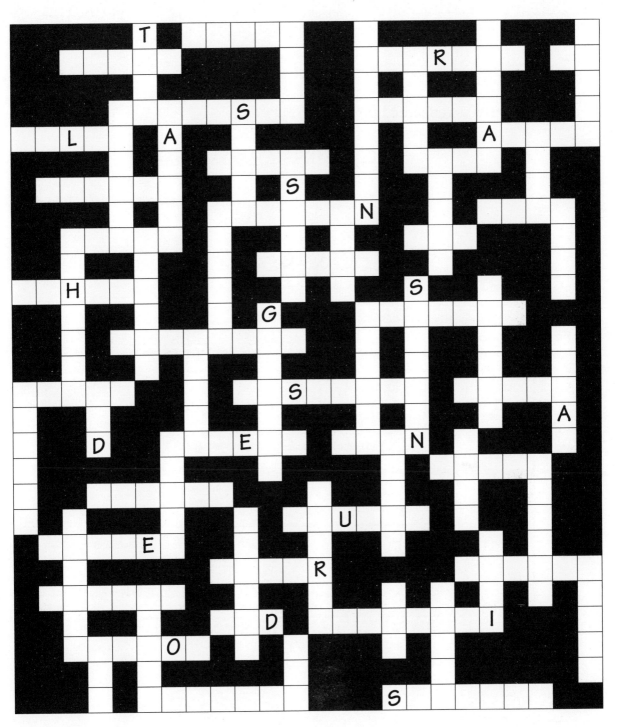

*E*ven grief is redeemed through Christ's love.

Clue: MESSIAH *is* YVNNAUZ

T J V N N V M   U C V

G Z X N V   F Z X

Y X Q C I'   K X C

G Z V E   N Z U J J

T V   L X Y K X C G V M.

There's a right time for everything. Fit words from Ecclesiastes 3:1–8 into the grid below. We've given you some letters as a start.

Unscramble the circled letters to complete this verse:

To everything there is a ___ ___ ___ ___ ___ ___, a time

for every ___ ___ ___ ___ ___ ___ ___ under heaven.

(Ecclesiastes 3:1)

Word Pool

**BORN   BREAK   BUILD   CAST   DANCE   DIE   EMBRACE   GAIN   GATHER   HATE
HEAL   KEEP   KILL   LAUGH   LOSE   LOVE   MOURN   PEACE   PLANT   PLUCK
REFRAIN   SEW   SILENCE   SPEAK   TEAR   THROW   WAR   WEEP**

Link the letters below in an unending string to reveal one of Jesus' greatest promises to us.

```
A    N    U    O    Y    D    N

D    S    A    W    D    K    I

I    T    K    N    I    F    N

I    W    K    A    L    L    O

L    B    E    S    U    C    U

L    E    E    O    K    O    M

G    V    Y    N    A    Y    A

E    I    O    D    O    T    T

N    T    T    I    T    E    H

I    W    B    E    P    D    W

L    L    E    O    N    E    7:7
```

Hezekiah's Tunnel

King Hezekiah led his people in a revolt against Sennacherib. In preparation for war, he strengthened his forces and defenses internally and made alliances against Assyria. He also assured the supply of water to Jerusalem by closing off the outlet of the Gihon spring (outside the walls of Jerusalem). The spring water was diverted by means of a tunnel to the Pool of Siloam (inside the city walls). (See 2 Kings 20:20.)

The tunnel was an engineering feat in its day. Two groups began digging at opposite ends of the proposed tunnel route, and after a mid-course correction, they met with only a few inches of adjustment required.

Work this maze from both directions.

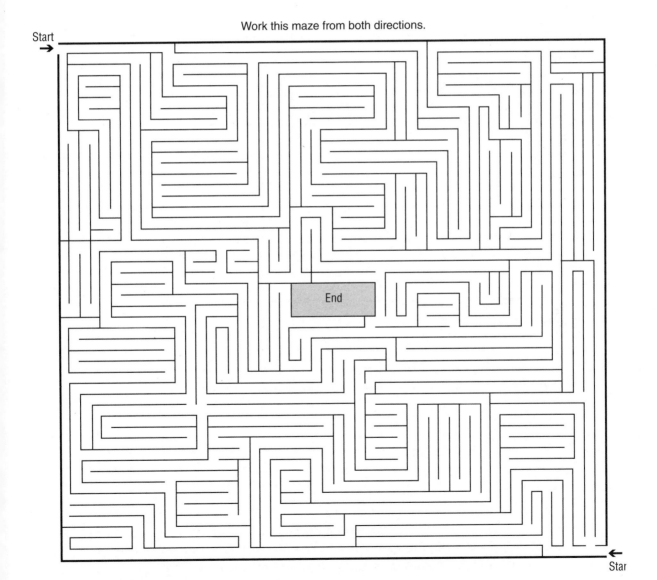

Start →

End

← Star

24

Scripture uses the metaphor of marriage to illustrate the relationship between God and His people. Below is a list of scrambled words from the Bible that all pertain to marriage. Unscramble the words to reveal the relationship of all Christians to Christ. Then unscramble the circled letters to reveal Christ's invitation to each person.

VINEIT

DANBUSH

FEWI

BOARNHOLE

DERBI

SIKS

DEWGNID

STAFE

VOLE

TGIF

RUCHCH

DERTHBOTE

GOMOREDIRB

CENTSAIDIF

STUGSE

SENTMARG

(Matthew 22:4)

Scripture Pool

Matthew 22:9–11   1 Corinthians 7:14   Luke 1:27   John 3:29   Genesis 29:11

John 2:2, 9   Ephesians 5:22, 25   Psalm 45:12   Hebrews 13:4

Find all twelve tribes of Israel in the puzzle below. The names run in all directions.

P N I M A J N E B W I R J K L

O A S D F G H J K H L R M O S

J P E M I A R H P E A X J I O

Y H X C E R J I W O T D S E W

B O J E R T D X I O H K U S E

N M R A H C A S S I P A N J R

M R O E S I N O P E A M U I D

F E G H U S I M E O N O L E S

I U S G H B K S I E W O U S L

I G E O D G E R E H S A B I R

R D L A E S T N M O P S E S E

P M G H E S S A N A M P Z P I

Most of the clues and answers to this crossword are based on the person, work, and ministry of the Holy Spirit.

Across

1 Petition on behalf of another
6 He sent the Spirit
11 Make evident, reveal
12 Male person
13 The Spirit knows what to pray for according to God's ____
15 Guarantee
17 Daddy
20 The Spirit gives ____
22 The Spirit is Jesus' ____ in the believer
24 The Spirit ____ Jesus into the wilderness to be tempted
25 Los Angeles (abbr.)
27 Those who were "with one accord" in one place described the coming of the Spirit as a mighty ____

30 Testify

32 Lines (abbr.)

34 The Spirit was sent to show us Jesus and ____ Him

35 Counselor

37 By the Spirit we know that we belong to ____

38 Jesus' ministry inaugurated the ____ of God

42 Extinguish

45 Instruct; one of the functions of the Spirit

46 Not cold

47 Presents

49 Symbol of the Holy Spirit

50 Flank

53 Sinful nature

55 For Jews, a feast day of the firstfruits

57 The Holy Spirit told Simeon he would ____ the Christ before he died

58 Like Father, like Son

59 The Spirit moved upon the face of the waters at ____

61 The Holy Spirit gives us ____ to live the new life in Christ

63 Northeast (abbr.)

64 Gift of the Spirit to bring wholeness

66 He that searches the heart, knows the ____ of the Spirit

67 Time between the Resurrection and Pentecost: seven ____

68 The Spirit enables believers to fulfill the great commission to ____ into all the world

Down

1 Living within

2 Speak, declare

3 Jesus went away so He could send the ____

4 Transgression

5 Father, Son, Holy Spirit: ____ God

7 By the Holy Spirit we have ____ to the Father

8 We are renewed in the ____ #12 Across

9 The Bible says this man was full of the Holy Ghost

10 Appeared in the shape of cloven tongues

12 Evidence of God's reign

14 The Holy Spirit gives an abundance of this in our hearts

16 Three in one

18 Water, fire, and Spirit

19 Wonder, amazement

21 Elisabeth, Zacharias, and John were all ____ with the Holy Spirit

23 Sagacity

26 Everything

28 If you live after the flesh, you ____

29 Fruit of the Spirit

30 Fuse

31 Conditional

33 The Spirit guides into all ____

34 The Holy Spirit is the #20 Across -____

35 In what way

36 Name for the Holy Spirit

39 Sadden

40 Flowing out

41 We become God's #43 Down by ____

43 As ____, then heirs

44 A Christian's ____ is not disappointed

48 Change your mind

50 High frequency (abbr.)

51 Ask, seek, ____

52 Our bodies are the ____ of God

54 At His baptism, Jesus received anointing for ministry, and assurance as God's ____

56 Frequent

60 Those who were filled with the Holy Spirit were not drunk with ____ wine

62 Brings death

65 The "Men of Galilee" saw Jesus ____ into Heaven before He sent the Holy Spirit

Unscramble the related words below and then unscramble the circled letters to reveal God's special delivery agency.

BEALGRI Ⓞ __ __ __ __ __ __

HRBIUCME __ __ __ __ __ __ Ⓞ

HSEETVLYNHOA __ __ __ __ __ Ⓞ __ __ __ __ Ⓞ __ (2 words)

CELAHIM __ __ __ __ __ Ⓞ __

ARNCAGHLE __ __ __ __ __ __ __ Ⓞ __

REFICUL __ __ __ __ __ Ⓞ __

RSHAMPIE Ⓞ __ Ⓞ __ __ __ __ __

__ __ __ __ __ __ __ __ __

Sackcloth and ashes are not exactly party fare, but the results could cause rejoicing.

Clue: MESSIAH *is* ZBMMTDE

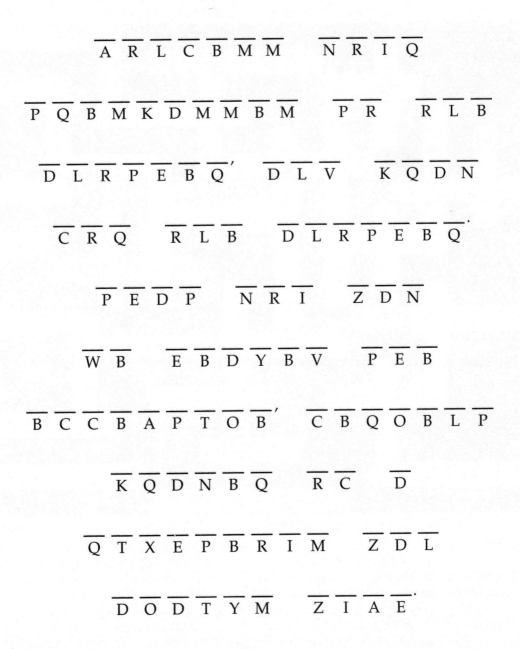

CONFESS YOUR

TRESPASSES TO ONE

ANOTHER' AND PRAY

FOR ONE ANOTHER.

THAT YOU MAY

BE HEALED THE

EFFECTIVE' FERVENT

PRAYER OF A

RIGHTEOUS MAN

AVAILS MUCH.

*H*as there ever been a more faithful daughter-in-law than Ruth? When Naomi's husband and children passed on, leaving her all alone, it was Ruth who willingly left her home and said to Naomi, "Your people shall be my people, and your God, my God." God recognized Ruth's selflessness and gave her a new husband—and made her part of the genealogy of Jesus Christ. Refer to your New King James Bible to find any answers you don't know.

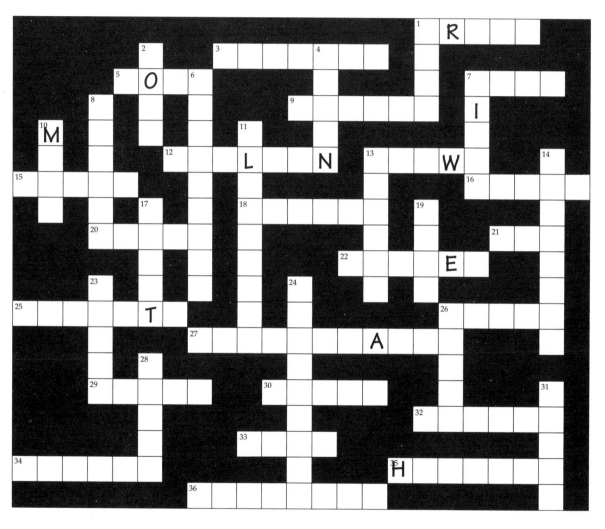

Across

1 Naomi's other daughter-in-law

3 At mealtime during the gathering of crops, Ruth dipped part of her loaf in this condiment

5 Naomi, her husband, and her sons moved here from #6 Down because of #8 Down

7 Following Naomi's instructions, Ruth went to the threshing floor and placed herself at her future husband's ____, and waited for him to tell her what she should do

9 Ruth deserved one of these for being so faithful to Naomi

12 Ruth's brother-in-law

13 Ruth used this garment to carry home food from the threshing floor

15 Oats are one

16 Ruth's great grandson

18 Ruth's husband

20 A dry measure equal to from three-eighths to two-thirds of a bushel

21 How many elders observed the transaction that resulted in Ruth's remarriage?

22 One of the two "cereals" that Ruth gathered by following the reapers

25 #2 Down told Ruth that when she felt this way, she should "go to the vessels" and partake of what the young men had drawn

26 Naomi's hometown was in the land of _____

27 #11 Down's nearest kinsman would have been forced to pass this up if he had exercised his option on #11 Down's property

29 This tragedy in the family was one reason that Naomi wanted to return to her homeland. (The other reason was that "the Lord had visited His people" in giving them food; #8 Down was over.)

30 Ruth sought refuge under these, belonging to the Lord God of Israel

32 According to Israel's law, the nearest relative was given the opportunity to do this with his late kinsman's property before any other relative could

33 Naomi lost two of them

34 The meaning of the name that Naomi took when she returned home (see #10 Down)

35 Naomi and Ruth arrived home at the beginning of this "time of gathering up crops"

36 Naomi sought this for Ruth, "that it may be well with you"; a good husband could provide it

Down

1 Ruth's son

2 Ruth's second husband

4 To go along behind the reapers and pick up the parts of the crop they drop or miss

6 Naomi's hometown, it was later the birthplace of one of Ruth's descendants

7 Where the seeds were planted

8 It drove Naomi and her family from their hometown

10 The name that Naomi took when she returned to her hometown

11 Naomi's husband

13 In Israel, taking this off signified that a deal had been made

14 The hour at which #2 Down awoke and found Ruth at the end of his pallet

17 The second of two "cereals" that Ruth gathered by following the reapers

19 Naomi's "condition" when she left her hometown; it expresses "having it all"

23 This is the foodstuff that God restored to His people when the land was fertile and productive once more

24 Being a Moabitess, Ruth was considered one of these in Naomi's hometown

26 Ruth's grandson

28 Ruth found this with her late father-in-laws kinsman; it meant food on Naomi's table

31 Naomi originally left her hometown as #19 Down, but returned this way

Unscramble the original given letters to find a descriptive word for Naomi:

___ ___ ___ ___ ___ ___ - ___ ___ - ___ ___ ___

*T*ry to solve the equation below without consulting the Scriptures!

The number of days after birth a male child was to be circumcised

_____

The number of days journey from Horeb by way of Mount Seir unto Kadesh-Barnea

×   _____

The number of days the children of Israel wept for Moses in the plains of Moab

+   _____

The number of days Jesus stayed with the Samaritans at Sychar

+   _____

The number of days Lazarus was in the tomb before Jesus called him back to life

÷   _____

The number of days Moses was on the mountain with the Lord God

+   _____

The number of days between the time Nabal's heart "died within him" and the time he actually died

−   _____

The number of days the "prince of the kingdom of Persia" withstood the heavenly messenger who came to interpret Daniel's vision

+   _____

The number of days required to build Nehemiah's wall

−   _____

The number of days set aside for celebrating Purim

+   _____

The number of days the Lord God took to complete His creation

−   _____

The number of Joseph's brothers who went to buy grain in Egypt

+   _____

The number of days it took Paul and his disciples to sail from Philippi to Troas

+   _____

The number of days it rained on the earth at the time of the Great Flood

=   _____

Unscramble the related words below to reveal the identity of an Old Testament judge.

TALETB __ __ __ __ __ (O)

DANESMIITI __ __ (O) __ __ (O) __ __ __ __

PGA (O) __ __

HUOST __ __ (O) __ __

PAMSL __ __ __ __ __

ICHETRPS __ (O) __ __ __ __ __ __

FECELES __ __ __ __ __ __ __

__ __ __ __ __ __

SIGNIFICANT SEVENS

*A*lthough Bible scholars do not all agree on the significance of the number *seven* in the Scripture, there is little doubt that it has played a frequent role in God's dealing with man. From the seven days of creation in Genesis to the seven seals in Revelation, the number occurs in nearly every book of the Bible. Some of the most memorable occurrences include the seven loaves, which at Jesus' hand fed the multitude and then filled seven baskets; the year of Jubilee which followed seven cycles of seven years; the seven times the Israelites marched around the walls of Jericho; and the seven statements of Christ from the cross.

Travel any direction to an adjacent block with the number seven from beginning to end.

↓ Start

7	6	5	3	2	5	1	6	7	7	7	9	4	9	5	0	2	7	1	4	7	7	5	9	4	0
0	7	7	9	7	8	7	4	2	1	7	7	7	0	7	8	7	7	5	6	1	7	7	7	6
7	9	5	0	7	0	7	0	3	3	4	8	0	1	7	7	3	2	7	0	4	3	2	0	3	7
7	6	3	1	8	2	6	7	0	4	9	6	5	2	8	6	7	5	7	7	2	7	1	9	1	7
4	7	7	4	4	7	5	7	7	0	8	6	5	7	4	6	7	9	2	8	7	7	8	0	7	3
2	1	5	7	6	7	7	0	9	7	5	7	7	9	7	0	2	7	5	4	7	9	2	7	4	2
1	5	7	3	9	8	7	4	3	2	7	1	6	8	5	7	3	7	6	7	5	2	7	3	1	6
6	7	0	4	5	8	3	8	6	2	1	7	0	2	3	7	9	1	7	7	8	5	0	7	7	7
2	8	1	7	7	7	9	7	7	5	0	1	7	9	8	7	4	9	7	3	2	0	4	7	5	0
2	1	4	7	6	0	7	8	9	7	5	8	0	8	7	4	1	7	3	7	9	5	4	7	1	4
3	7	9	3	7	5	3	1	3	7	6	3	1	9	7	5	6	5	0	8	7	2	7	9	5	0
7	7	2	2	7	4	7	5	7	6	8	4	7	7	6	7	3	1	7	7	3	4	1	7	2	0
7	4	2	7	2	4	6	7	3	5	4	7	3	8	0	7	4	7	0	4	9	5	8	7	5	2
3	3	4	7	0	0	2	7	1	5	0	7	4	9	1	7	1	7	2	8	3	6	7	7	7	7
4	0	2	5	7	6	9	7	2	4	7	8	5	8	7	0	2	4	0	7	0	7	9	2	3	9
7	7	7	7	3	8	5	7	7	8	4	7	7	9	2	3	1	8	0	7	3	5	7	7	4
1	2	5	0	7	4	1	3	9	5	6	2	4	9	5	7	4	2	9	7	3	8	3	0	7	9
5	7	7	4	7	7	7	7	7	8	0	1	7	8	9	7	7	4	7	0	7	7	7	2	7	0
7	6	9	0	5	8	2	8	7	5	3	7	5	7	8	2	4	7	5	3	8	5	7	9	7	3
7	5	6	7	7	7	1	7	4	7	7	2	3	9	7	7	7	3	7	2	5	1	7	7	4	0
7	7	7	7	5	9	7	5	9	0	4	6	7	7	1	2	0	5	0	7	2	7	3	9	7	7

↑ End

MORE THAN CONQUERORS

God knows the attacks, temptations, and the enemies that come against Christians. He knows what it takes to defeat the enemy, so He has equipped the believers with the "armor of God." To quench the fiery darts of the wicked one, Christians are given, above all, the shield of faith. (See Ephesians 6:14-17.)

How is it that the shield of faith defends against the enemy? Just what is it that Christians receive by their faith for the defense of soul and spirits? The Bible says that by faith we have salvation, justifications, pure hearts, peace, joy, everlasting life, access to God, healing, and victory that overcomes the world. By faith, Christians have all they need to be more than conquerors.

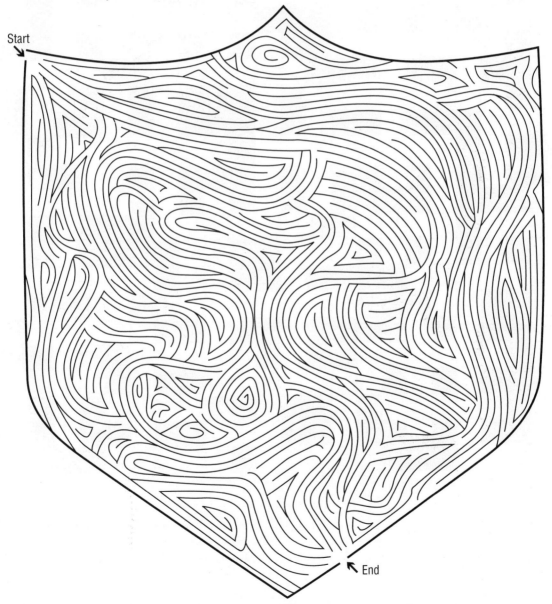

Start

End

The Kingdom of Heaven is like . . . fill in the answers with clues pertaining to the Kingdom of Heaven and Jesus' parables on the Kingdom.

Across

1 Stories with more than one level of meaning

4 When the wood, hay, and stubble are burned up, this will be left

6 Planted

10 The cost of the pearl of great price

12 Desire, search out

14 Atmosphere

15 Those who accept the invitation

16 Southeast (abbr.)

18 Friend

19 God's provision of righteousness for wedding #15 Across

21 This seed makes the point that inauspicious beginnings don't determine success or failure

24 What we'd call the men in Matthew 22:6

25 Those who think they are first may be in for this surprise

27 This person knew real value when he saw it

30 Land-____

31 Affirmative (bibl.)

32 A day's wages

33 Day of Judgment

36 Leading edge (abbr.)

39 Sows bad seeds

41 Time

43 This was stored in vessels; the rest was tossed out

45 In the Kingdom of Heaven, God rules in our ____

47 If this functions properly, you are blessed

48 Associate Arts degree (abbr.)

49 Yeast

51 Near (abbr.)

52 Message of Jesus' forerunner

54 Pronoun without gender

55 Hell

57 Fruit of the #67 Across

59 Jesus revealed what had been ____

61 Wringing of hands, tearing one's hair, #15 Down of ____

62 Maidens

65 Hearts and taskmasters

67 Ground

68 A bird's home

69 Not new

71 Exchanged for something else of value

72 Rule

73 Discovered

74 Ancient name for God

Down

1 Jesus spoke in #1 Across', fulfilling __

2 Domain

3 God's winged creatures

5 Everyone who __will be given more

7 These women heeded the motto: "Be prepared"

8 The expected One

9 Sons of the Kingdom or of the wicked one

11 Smallest

13 Peter was given the __ (sing.) of the Kingdom

15 What the tormented do

17 In the ____, the weeds and the wicked will meet their ____

20 Only God can shed some light on these

22 Good stewards put their #35 Down to good ____

23 The heart and this are in the same place

26 ____ of Man sows good seed

27 A large number are called

28 9:00 AM; ____ hour

29 Where treasure was hidden

32 This was full of good and bad

34 Not everyone who has #47 Across can ____

35 Gifts, abilities

37 Those who are involved in this have no place in the Kingdom

38 The far reaches of the Kingdom

40 Wicked

42 Estimated time of arrival (abbr.)

44 Wedding feast fare

45 This activity should result in understanding

46 Offspring of the wicked one

50 Where there is work to be done

53 If you have this, you can pay attention

56 If the #47 Across and #53 Down don't function, and the #45 Across (sing.) is #65 Across it will be difficult to know this

57 Select few

58 Gem

60 Television (abbr.)

61 Tennessee (abbr.)

63 Unprofitable

64 Image

66 Not sharp

70 Damage free (abbr.)

*I*n the box of letters below find seven things at which the Queen of Sheba marveled when she came to see King Solomon.

```
L   O   M   B   I   C   S   T   E   I   P   O

S   E   R   V   D   O   M   E   T   O   R   S

W   Y   R   O   H   E   S   E   O   H   I   R

I   S   A   A   E   W   I   S   D   O   M   E

S   O   N   T   P   T   N   A   V   U   W   R

V   I   S   C   U   P   B   E   A   S   P   A

A   C   O   S   T   N   A   V   R   E   S   E

E   H   U   A   E   B   M   S   P   A   P   B

N   C   E   D   S   I   W   A   C   P   V   P

T   M   H   E   M   O   D   E   O   E   R   U

S   O   C   R   T   G   N   R   S   E   N   C

H   M   O   P   R   A   E   B   R   E   S   T
```

*T*his Bible verse, found in the New Testament, is a familiar one. It's one of God's promises that ultimately means the end of the old life and the beginning of the new. (Hint: There's no code number for the letter "Z"—you won't need it. And to make this a little more difficult, the words are scrambled; they form two sentences.)

Clue: MESSIAH *is* 3 5 4 4 4 1 3

Unscramble the letters:

```
__ __ __ __ __     __ __ __ __ __ __     __ __ __     __ __ __ __
4  5  1  4  4      1  4  5  5  4  5      1  4  4      3  5  3  5

          __ __ __ __ __     __ __ __     __ __     __ __ __ __
          5  1  5  4  4      3  4  3      3  5      4  5  5  3

__ __     __ __ __ __ __ __     __ __ __ __     __ __ __ __ __
3  5      2  5  3  5  2  4      3  4  2  2      2  5  4  3  5

     __ __     __ __ __     __ __ __ __     __     __ __ __ __
     1  5      1  4  4      4  5  5  3      4      3  4  5  3

__ __ __ __ __     __ __ __     __ __     __ __     __ __ __ __
1  4  5  3  1      5  3  5      3  5      4  1      3  4  5  3

          __ __ __ __     __ __ __     __ __     __ __ __
          4  4  4  5      5  3  5      5  5      1  4  4

     __ __ __     __     __ __ __ __ __     __ __     __ __ __
     1  4  4      4      3  5  1  3  4      4  4      3  4  3
```

Unscramble the words:

_____

_____

_____

_____

_____

37

*T*here was no retirement for Sarah, the wife of Abraham. At an age when most women were bouncing great grandchildren on their knees, Sarah was still waiting to have her first child. Her doubts were many, but as we read her story in Genesis, her underlying faith in God comes through. God kept His promise, and Sarah and Abraham took their place in the bloodline that led to the birth of Jesus Christ.

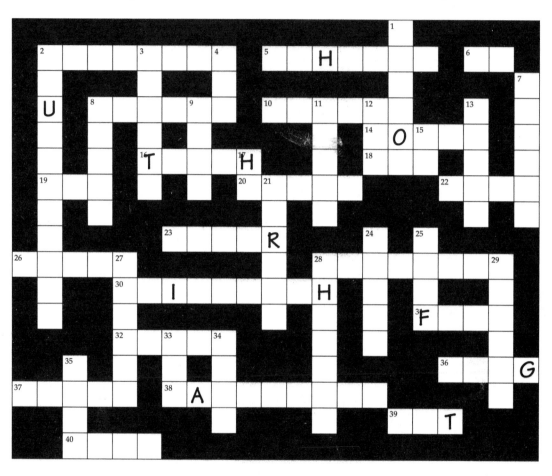

Across

2 God's agreement with Abraham

5 The "surrogate heir"

6 As God was known to the patriarchs in Old Testament times: ____ Shaddai

8 The land where Sarah and Abraham resided; it was God's gift to them

10 She really was this to her husband, by half

14 The women of the house of #30 Across found theirs closed because of Sarah

16 Sarah's father-in-law

18 Of God's agreement with Abraham, there would be no ____

19 Sarah was pleasing to it

20 Abraham's original name, meaning "exalted father"

22 Sarah was buried in this

23 Sarah gave this woman to her husband to be his wife when she herself could not conceive

26 In the wilderness on the way to Shur, he is the

one who comforted the mother of Abraham's first child after she fled from Sarah's presence

28 Because of his fondness for Sarah, Pharaoh didn't make Abraham wait for some of these

30 God talked in his sleep and kept him from touching Sarah, then this ruler gave Abraham some valuable property and money and returned Sarah to him

31 Abraham had to pay for Sarah's final resting place. How many hundred shekels of silver did he give to Ephron?

32 The town that #30 Across ruled

36 Long may he reign

37 Abraham couldn't count them, can you?

38 Location of the field where Sarah, Abraham, Isaac, Rebekah, Jacob, and Leah were buried; it was the only property the patriarchs owned (that is, purchased) in the Promised Land

39 The son of Abraham's brother Haran

40 This document, confirming Abraham's ownership of Sarah's burial place, was a good one

Down

1 The city where Sarah died

2 Sarah's was so beautiful, Abraham passed her off as a sibling

3 Sarah was over ____ years old when her son was born

4 How long had Abraham and Sarah lived in the Promised Land when Abraham's first son was born?

7 "Morsels" of money

8 Taxi of the desert; Abraham received this type of animal from Pharaoh

9 A unit of measure for Abraham's inheritance from God

11 Sarah's original name also meant "princess"

12 You could accuse her of wool-gathering; she figured in the oath that Abraham made with #30 Across

13 God's promise fulfilled

15 Is there one in the house? (abbr.)

17 What Sarah might have exclaimed at the thought of conceiving a child at her age

21 It turned out to be a temporary (albeit long-lived) condition for Sarah

24 #30 Across had one that saved his life

25 Sarah didn't cook this animal for their heavenly visitors; she was busy making cakes

27 Sarah giggles

28 These were a standard unit of weight in Old Testament times

29 Refreshing water was available at this spot in the wilderness; Sarah's servant found solace there

33 A mate for #12 Down. He was part of the proof that Abraham would inherit the Promised Land

34 #22 Across probably had walls made of this

35 She waited on Sarah while Sarah waited on God

Unscramble the given letters to reveal the means by which Sarah received strength to conceive seed:

___ ___ ___ ___ ___ ___ ___   ___ ___ ___ ___ ___

(Hebrews 11:11)

Old orders stand until new orders arrive.

Clue: MESSIAH *is* DVJJZRY

X F   K Y V I V W F I V   R E U

D R B V   U Z J T Z G C V J   F W

R C C   E R K Z F E J '   S R G K Z Q Z E X

K Y V D   Z E   K Y V   E R D V   F W

K Y V   W R K Y V I   R E U   F W

K Y V   J F E   R E U   F W   K Y V

Y F C P   J G Z I Z K '   K V R T Y Z E X

K Y V D   K F   F S J V I M V   R C C

K Y Z E X J   K Y R K   Z   Y R M V

T F D D R E U V U   P F L ;   R E U   C F

Z   R D   N Z K Y   P F L   R C N R P J

V M V E   K F   K Y V   V E U

F W   K Y V   R X V .

CHOSEN BRIDE

*T*o find just the right bride for his beloved son Isaac, the aging Abraham sent his trusted servant off to his homeland of Mesopotamia. The servant loaded up ten camels with some of Abraham's best things and began the journey. When he arrived, he felt the full weight of his task, and he prayed, "O Lord God of my master Abraham, please give me success this day, and show kindness to my master Abraham. . . . Now let it be that the young woman to whom I say, 'Please let down your pitcher that I may drink,' and she says, 'Drink, and I will also give your camels a drink' — let her be the one You have appointed for Your servant Isaac" (Genesis 24:12, 14).

Before he was even through praying, beautiful Rebekah came out with her water pitcher. He asked for a drink of water and she agreed. Then she offered to draw water for the camels. It didn't take this servant long to realize his prayers for his master had been answered. After Abraham's servant made arrangements with Rebekah's family, she made the journey back to the land of Canaan to become Isaac's wife and the mother of his children, continuing the lineage of Abraham.

Start

End

*H*e's best known for "dry bones," but Ezekiel was a prophet whose words we would be wise to heed, even in this day. When God chooses a people, makes a covenant, and pours out His blessings upon them, what should their response be? What is *our* response to the God who loves and blesses and keeps and saves us? This puzzle deals with the entire book of Ezekiel; use the New King James Version to find the answers.

Across

1 The priests couldn't drink this in the inner court of the temple

8 The foolish prophets of Ezekiel's day gave this type of vision; it was useless

9 One of the six men in one of Ezekiel's visions carried this writer's implement at his side

10 Ezekiel found the scroll of this surprisingly tasty

11 God sought a man to make a wall and stand in the ____ before Him on behalf of Israel; there was no one

14 God promised to leave this after destroying most of the people of Israel

15 As men gather bronze, iron, ____, and other metals, and place them in a furnace, God will put Israel there to burn

16 God said He would bring Tyre down with those who descend into the ____

21 To sustain Ezekiel when he was symbolizing the years of Israel's and Judah's iniquity, God allowed him this amount of water: one-sixth of a ____

22 People who came to Ezekiel heard his words but ignored them. With their mouths they showed ____, but their hearts pursued their own gain

24 The prophets' visions were like building a boundary wall and plastering it with untempered ____; it will fall

26 Contraction for I am

28 God told Ezekiel to do this to his head and beard

29 In viewing the temple abominations, Ezekiel saw____ men of the elders with censers in their hands

30 When Ezekiel fell on his face before God, God commanded him to "____"!

33 Editor (abbr.)

35 This bird was used to symbolize Nebuchadnezzar, who carried away Israel's princes

36 God pressed Ezekiel to take this type of plate and set it as a wall between him and the city

37 God will spread His net over the prince in Jerusalem and catch him in His ____, like an animal

38 The king of Babylon used divination: shook arrows, consulted images, and looked at the ____ (without X-rays!)

40 Ezekiel's father

44 Five of the six men from #9 Across slew old and young men, little children, and ____

46 Article

47 The man from #9 Across scattered coals of ____ over the city

48 Ezekiel was to bake his cakes by using human waste for fuel; it was a sign of eating this type of bread among the Gentiles, where God would drive His people

49 In the valley of dry bones, God put ____ and flesh on the bones

51 Shepherds who fed themselves should have been feeding their ____

54 After his initial vision, Ezekiel went to the captives at this place and sat, astonished

55 The land of God's people was ruled with crimes and ____; none bothered to wipe it up

57 One of the four faces of the living creatures

58 Either . . . ____.

59 When God executes judgment, one-third of the people will die by this

60 The elders had these in their hearts, not the true God

62 The scroll contained writings of lamentations, mourning, and ____

63 One of three well-known men of God who could have saved only himself in the unfaithful land of Ezekiel's day

65 Moab, ____, and Phillstia would see the vengeance of God

66 This tribe received two portions of the land—for Ephraim and Manasseh

68 God said He'd put these in Gog's jaws and lead him out

69 When the land was divided by lots into inheritance, a ____ was set apart for God—a holy portion

71 God will make Rabbah, the Ammonites' city, a stable for this animal

72 Priests had to change these before leaving the temple's holy chamber (sing.)

73 Israel would become one ____ with one king

74 Men took one of these in exchange for killing

Down

1 The living creatures had four of these

2 A standard unit of measure, it equaled 17½ to 20 inches

3 Priests' clothes had to be made of this fabric

4 God said He'd purge these "unmanageables" from among His people; they wouldn't enter Israel

5 Another name for Samaria, meaning "She of the Tent"

6 One of the people that would judge Jerusalem, along with Babylonia and other Chaldeans

7 On His holy mountain, God will accept His people as a sweet ____ to His nose

12 Egyptians are originally from the land of ____

13 God's people were held ____ by numerous nations

17 Israel played harlot with the Egyptians and Assyrians and erected a ____ at the head of every road

18 God will knock the ____ out of Gog's left hand and arrows from his right

19 In an early vision, Ezekiel saw the walls of the temple, with creeping things, abominable ____ (sing.), and idols portrayed there

20 The six men of #9 Across each had a deadly weapon: A ____-ax.

23 How many months it would take Israel to bury Gog and his multitude

25 Another name for Jerusalem, meaning "My tent is in her."

27 The trees on the river bank near the restored temple had fruit for food and leaves for ____, for healing

31 At the end of the book: The name of the city shall be "The Lord is ____"

32 Another of the men from #63 Across

34 The people of God who survive destruction will escape to the mountains, like this bird of the valleys

39 Ezekiel was sent to the children of Israel because they were ____; they wouldn't obey God

41 The sons of ____ of the tribe of Levi could approach God

42 A priest could marry another priest's widow, or a ____

43 God said He would leave His people in the furnace to "become liquid"

45 The gateway of the temple's inner court (facing east) was only open on the Sabbath and the day of the ____ (two words)

50 When God gathers His scattered children, He will replace their hearts of stone with hearts of ____

52 Gog will come like a ____ to cover the Israelites' land

53 This city that burned was less corrupt than older sister Israel

55 When Gog comes, every man's weapon will be against this close relative

56 The house of Israel had become ____ from silver; it was impure

61 Those who survive God's punishment will have ____ hands and knees as weak as water

64 The taste of the scroll was like this sweet substance

66 God lifted His hand in oath to descendants of the house of ____ on the day He chose Israel

67 When His people seek____, they'll find none—only anxiety

70 An offering for the prince of Israel would be one lamb from a flock of how many hundred?

THE MOLINE CROSS

*E*ach arm of the Moline Cross ends in two graceful, outward-curving petals. The resemblance to the crossed iron, or moline, of the upper millstone is what gives this cross design its name.

The arms of the cross seem to evoke an all-embracing, far-reaching feeling, and thus the cross is frequently associated with the Great Commission: "Go therefore and make disciples of all the nations, baptizing them in the name of the Father and of the Son and of the Holy Spirit, teaching them to observe all things that I have commanded you; and lo, I am with you always, even to the end of the age" (Matthew 28:19–20).

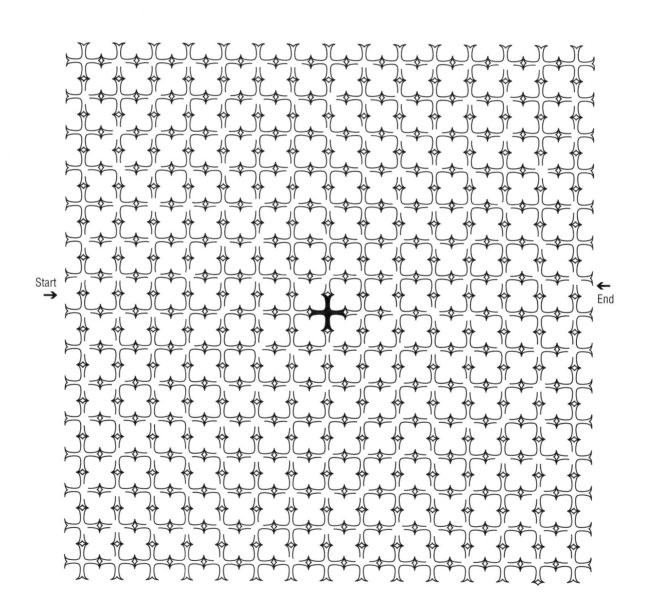

Start →

← End

*J*esus was asked the question, "Who do You think You are?" In the letter grid find 16 "I AMs" of Jesus.

R	R	O	O	T	O	F	D	A	V	I	D	Y
E	A	S	O	F	F	S	P	R	I	N	G	E
M	P	H	W	E	R	F	H	A	C	E	W	F
B	R	E	A	D	O	F	L	I	F	E	B	I
I	L	P	T	R	E	S	V	E	R	Y	R	L
O	L	H	Y	T	H	G	I	M	L	A	A	H
O	N	E	Z	E	I	N	E	S	G	H	T	T
D	I	R	N	T	I	A	M	E	P	A	S	U
R	O	D	H	I	O	N	M	L	S	E	G	R
U	G	G	W	E	V	O	A	T	R	A	N	T
F	I	G	R	S	A	E	W	O	R	K	I	Y
L	N	O	M	D	S	E	U	B	O	R	N	A
S	O	A	T	E	V	W	E	R	O	O	R	W
D	R	E	S	U	R	R	E	C	T	I	O	N
R	U	I	T	A	T	R	E	Y	A	R	M	D

Scripture Pool

John 6:35; 8:12, 58; 10:9, 11; 11:25; 14:6; 15:1; Revelation 1:8; 22:16

*T*he books of the Old Testament provide the answers to this crossword.

Across

3 The temple rebuilt
4 The book of the weeping prophet
5 Prophesied the birthplace of the Messiah
6 Jerusalem plundered and Edom's demise
8 The prophet during the Babylonian exile
10 The crossing, the conquest, and the land
11 The people spared and the Feast of Purim begun
12 Return to the land
16 Book of praises
17 The wall is rebuilt
18 Loyalty rewarded
19 Nineveh's downfall
20 First book of the Pentateuch
24 In Hebrew, "The words, events, of the days"
26 Details laws on sacrifices
31 Wilderness wanderings
32 The shepherd prophet from Tekoa
33 This prophet's name means "My messenger"
34 Love story

Down

1 Eight visions
2 The prophet voices complaints about evil and God's justice
4 The problem of suffering
7 The farewell address, the law reviewed and the eve of the entrance to Canaan
9 Odes of woe
10 Prophesied the outpouring of the Spirit on all people
13 Central theme is the coming "Day of the Lord" that will bring destruction
14 End of the judges and the kingdom established
15 The one that (almost) got away
21 The great escape
22 The preacher
23 Practical wisdom
25 The kingdom divided
27 True love spurned
28 Prophesied the suffering servant
29 From Joshua to Samuel
30 Dreams, visions, and uncompromising loyalty

Jesus said He came to fulfill the Law and the Prophets, not destroy them. Indeed, heaven and earth will disappear before the least of the commandments. Unscramble the circled letters to reveal what Jesus said those are:

___ ___ ___   ___ ___ ___   ___ ___ ___ ___ ___ ___

44

Wood was a popular material in Bible times. It was used to make a variety of items, such as . . . well, we aren't going to tell you what it was used for. It's up to you to figure that out in this puzzle. Unscramble the letters and spell out items made of wood, things built with wood, types of wood, and the forms wood takes. Then, unscramble the circled letters and spell out a New Testament verse that tells you what is "king of the hill," so to speak.

DANHANWEOP
◯_◯_ _◯_ _ _ _
(2 words)

FATFS _◯_ _ _

SLESEVS ◯_ _ _◯_ _

KAR ◯_ _

SOSRC _ _◯_ _

SOLID _ _ _ _◯

ROODS ◯_ _ _ _

ARCT _◯_◯

EIRF ◯_ _ _

RLOOSF _ _ _◯_ _

COBKL _◯_ _ _

KEYSO _◯_ _◯

LOPES _ _ _◯_

BATSO _ _ _◯_

SARB _◯_ _

POCANY _◯_ _ _ _

WOBS _◯_ _

BURCHIME _◯_ _ _◯_ _

GAMERN _ _ _ _◯_

RACEVDGAMEI
_ _ _◯_ _ _ _ _ _◯
(2 words)

PETMEL _◯_ _ _◯

DOGS _ _ _◯

WARSRO _ _◯_ _◯

TARMLOFP _ _ _◯◯_ _ _

BEATL ◯_ _ _ _

SWEIKSORGE _ _ _ _◯_ _ _ _ _

SLACIUMMIRTSETNUNS
_ _ _◯_ _ _
_ _ _◯_ _◯_ _ _ _
(2 words)

LAWLS ◯_ _ _

TALRA _ _◯_ _

FIRNGEOF ◯_ _ _ _◯_ _

BACELEARNT _ _◯_ _ _ _ _ _◯_

OLDEMDMAIEG _ _ _ _◯_ _ _ _◯_
(2 words)

PHISS _◯_ _ _

DAROSB _ _ _ _◯_

GIESTRHHNPELESTIMMN
_ _◯_ _◯_ _ _
◯_◯_ _ _◯_◯_
(2 words)

PEOHRG _ _ _◯◯_

QAPUALNNI _ _ _ _◯_◯_ _

RAILPLS _ _◯_ _◯_

Verse:

_ _ _   _ _ _   _ _ _ _ _   _ _ _ _   _ _ _ _   _ _ _ _
_ _ _ _   _ _ _ _ _   _ _ _   _ _ _   _ _ _ _ _ _ _
_ _   _ _ _ _ _   _ _   _ _ _ _

Solve the following puzzle by connecting adjacent letters (in all directions) to reveal how to experience God's leading.

T	L	T	I	W	O	E	S	T	A
H	L	H	D	R	H	L	R	D	N
E	I	A	(T)	T	D	E	I	I	N
N	H	I	N	R	N	N	G	H	A
R	A	E	T	U	U	N	Y	T	L
T	A	N	S	T	O	W	A	W	L
L	D	O	H	T	O	E	N	Y	S
E	N	T	N	I	N	W	O	K	A
A	N	U	D	E	L	S	H	A	C
H	E	G	N	H	E	E	R	D	L
I	M	A	D	(S)	T	T	C	I	L

	H	H		
	Y	T		
	P	A		

Jesus taught that the Sabbath is created for our benefit and should not interfere with our decision to help others. After all, the greatest commandment is to love God with all your heart and soul, and then to love your neighbor as yourself—no matter what day of the week it is.

Across

2 After sacrificing their "hope for the future" to their idols, the people of Israel profaned the Sabbath by entering the sanctuary on the same day

8 A woman, who had a spirit of infirmity for ____ years was healed on the Sabbath, raising the indignation of the synagogue's ruler

9 In the wilderness, the Israelites were supposed to bake and ____ whatever foods were needed for the Sabbath, on the day before the Sabbath

10 When the Shunammite woman's son died, her husband, unaware of the death, asked why she was going to see this man of God, since it wasn't the Sabbath

12 This unit of measure is how much manna the Israelites gathered on the sixth day: two ____ instead of one, to prepare for the Sabbath

15 When Jesus stood and read the Book of ____ in the synagogue on the Sabbath, He told the people that the Scriptures had been fulfilled in their hearing

16 At the Feast of Firstfruits, the priest waved one of these before the Lord on the Israelites' behalf, on the day after Sabbath, to signify the first harvest

19 Not out

20 The day before the Sabbath, ____ Day, Joseph of Arimathea asked for the body of Jesus

22 When Jesus taught in the synagogue on the Sabbath, the people were astonished, asking, "What ____ is this which is given to Him, this Son of Mary?"

25 At Philippi, Paul, Silas, and Timothy went on the Sabbath to the riverside where "conversation with God" was customarily made (pl.)

27 If the Israelites didn't break the Sabbath the way their fathers did, and if they heeded God, then kings and princes sitting on the throne of David and riding in these would enter the gates of their city, a city which would remain forever

30 At the end of seven Sabbatical cycles (49 years) came the year of ____: That entire year, the people could not sow crops or reap

31 For the Feast of Weeks, the grain offering was two wave loaves of fine flour, baked with this fermenting agent

33 Preaching on the Sabbath at #1 Down, Paul said those in Jerusalem and the rulers didn't know Jesus or the voice of these "men of God" that were ready every Sabbath (sing.)

34 How many years did the Promised Land lay fallow to make up for the years when the people refused to observe the Sabbath?

35 One of three divisions of the psyche

37 Although the Israelites gathered twice as much manna on the sixth day, the extra portion didn't stink or have any of these when they ate it on the Sabbath

38 Visiting the house of a Pharisee ruler to eat bread on the Sabbath, Jesus healed a man of this disease

39 During the land's Sabbath rest, the people could not reap what grew of its own accord, nor gather these from untended vines (sing.)

40 In the wilderness, a man who was caught gathering sticks on the Sabbath was taken out and ____ as a final punishment

Down

1 Paul and his party stopped in this city and, on the Sabbath, Paul stood and preached Jesus; after the Jews left the synagogue, the Gentiles wanted Paul to preach the same to them on the next Sabbath

3 On the same day as #22 Across, many were offended by Jesus, resulting in fewer healings. Jesus was indeed a #33 Across without ____ in His own country

4 God said the land would enjoy its Sabbaths while it lay ____ (lonely) without the Israelites

5 Blessed is the man who keeps from defiling the Sabbath and keeps his hand from doing any ____

6 The men of Tyre who lived in the area were guilty of bringing this to sell on the Sabbath in Jerusalem

7 The king of Assyria, Tiglath-____ contributed to #14 Down's disregard for God's temple

11 At the Pool of Bethesda by the ____ Gate, this man wasn't fuzzy about the healing he received at Jesus' hand on the Sabbath; his 38 years of sickness were over

13 "My Sabbaths you shall keep,"(NKJ) God said. It was "a ____ between Me and you," an indication that God sanctified them

14 This king removed the Sabbath pavilion that had been built in the temple, possibly due to the influence of the king of Assyria

17 The Israelites couldn't kindle any of these in their habitations on the Sabbath (sing.)

18 From the day after the seventh Sabbath after the Feast of Firstfruits, the Israelites counted ____ days and celebrated the Feast of Weeks with a new grain offering

19 The gateway of this court (facing east) would be closed on the six working days, but open on the Sabbath and the day of the New Moon

20 In Corinth, Paul stayed with Aquila and ____, and reasoned in the synagogue every Sabbath, persuading many Jews and Greeks

21 This was made for man, not man for it

23 Anyone who profaned the Sabbath would suffer a premature one

24 In a song for the Sabbath day (found In Psalms), God's lovingkindness and faithfulness should be declared on an instrument of ten strings, and on the ____ and the harp

26 If one of these animals fell into a pit on the Sabbath, Jesus asked, wouldn't the Pharisees lift it out? So is healing on the Sabbath a sin?

28 From Mount ____ to Jerusalem is a Sabbath day's journey. The disciples made the trip after Jesus ascended to Heaven

29 God told Moses to tell the Israelites to "keep My Sabbath and reverence My ____,"or "holy place where the Lord was present"

30 This priest brought together Queen Athaliah's officers and bodyguards to provide protection for the rightful heir, Joash, at his coronation

32 The man in #11 Down was told to take this up and walk, but the Jews told him it wasn't lawful to carry it on the Sabbath (pl.)

33 For six years, the Israelites were to sow the fields, and ____ the vineyard and gather its fruit; the seventh year was a Sabbath for the land

34 At the Sabbath sunset, the whole city gathered at the door of this disciple's house, and Jesus healed many and cast out demons

36 In Ezekiel, the priests had profaned holy things, and had hidden their ____ from God's Sabbaths

THE ANCHOR CROSS

*T*he writer to the Hebrews speaks of hope as "an anchor of the soul" (Hebrews 6:19). Thus, this cross design is also called the Cross of Hope.

The cross design was popular among early Christians. It has been associated especially with St. Clement, Bishop of Rome, who according to tradition was martyred under the Trajan persecutions by being bound to an anchor and cast into the sea.

Start

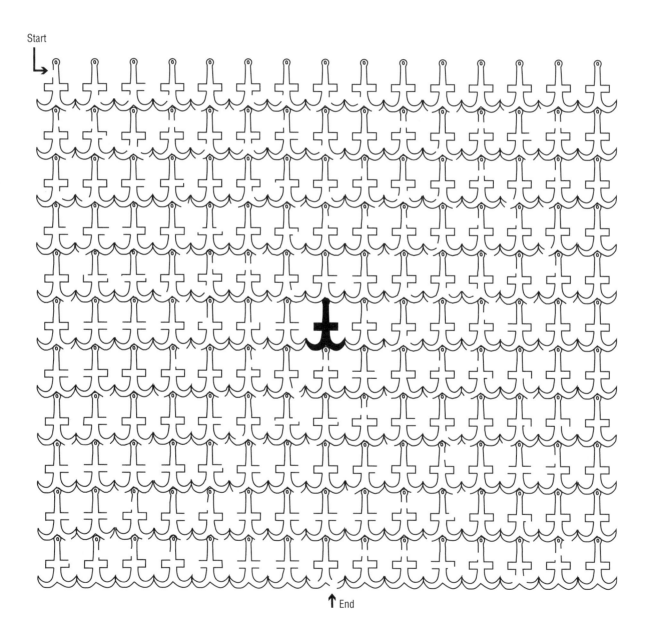

↑ End

There are many hidden treasures of great and precious value to be searched out in the Word of God. In the letter box below "dig out" the buried treasures of the shiny and glittering kind that are found in the Bible.

G	H	O	W	P	Z	B	T	R	E	V	X	L	M	W
E	T	A	G	A	X	R	O	O	D	L	O	G	Q	W
X	O	W	A	R	E	A	H	I	L	Y	R	E	B	Z
Z	P	W	S	B	V	S	O	S	N	N	P	P	R	R
S	A	R	D	I	U	S	T	A	M	B	E	R	O	R
O	Z	R	E	W	C	K	I	P	T	R	A	L	N	E
E	D	N	O	M	A	I	D	P	T	O	R	X	Z	L
A	N	Y	N	O	O	L	K	H	S	I	L	V	E	R
B	R	A	Y	C	A	L	E	I	T	N	O	P	T	L
T	O	X	X	R	A	R	M	R	H	E	T	S	I	K
S	A	R	E	W	P	A	M	E	T	H	Y	S	T	B
A	E	M	J	E	L	E	W	N	B	B	T	R	O	N
S	E	E	S	I	O	U	Q	R	U	T	T	S	U	R
M	H	T	N	I	C	A	J	R	G	T	E	A	C	G

Word Pool

AGATE   AMBER   AMETHYST   BERYL   BRASS   BRONZE
DIAMOND   EMERALD   GOLD   JACINTH   ONYX   PEARL
RUBY   SAPPHIRE   SARDIUS   SILVER   TOPAZ   TURQUOISE

*T*ry to solve the equation below without looking up the references! All of the figures are from the book of Leviticus.

The number of days and nights Aaron and his sons were commanded to abide at the door of the tabernacle for their consecration   _____

$+$ The number of the month in which the Day of Atonement falls on the Jewish calendar   _____

$\times$ The number of the day in the month on which the Day of Atonement falls   _____

$\times$ The number of the day on which the unconsumed portion of a peace offering was to be burned   _____

$\div$ The number of days each week in which work is to be done   _____

$+$ The day of the month in which Passover begins at evening   _____

$\div$ The number of loaves to be "waved" as an offering of firstfruits   _____

$+$ The number of the month that begins with a blowing of trumpets   _____

$+$ The number of the day in the month on which the feast of tabernacles begins   _____

$-$ The number of the month on the Jewish calendar in which Passover falls   _____

$\div$ The number of days the children of Israel were commanded to "dwell in booths"   _____

$-$ The number of birds to be brought for sacrifice by a leper at the time of his cleansing   _____

$=$ The number of the day that is "the Sabbath of the Lord"   _____

HUGS AND KISSES

*E*mbracing (or hugging) and kissing are customs that are noted thoughout the Bible. Among other things, biblical kisses were given as a blessing (Genesis 48:10–16), an anointing (1 Samuel 10:1), a sign of reconciliation (Genesis 33:4), and even a sign of false religion (1 Kings 19:18; Hosea 13:2). In Jesus' parable of the prodigal son, the kiss of the father to his son symbolized not only the great joy of reunion, but also forgiveness and acceptance. But perhaps the most well-known kiss in the Bible is the one by which Jesus was betrayed (Luke 22:47–48).

Travel any direction to an adjacent block with an X to get from one kiss to the other.

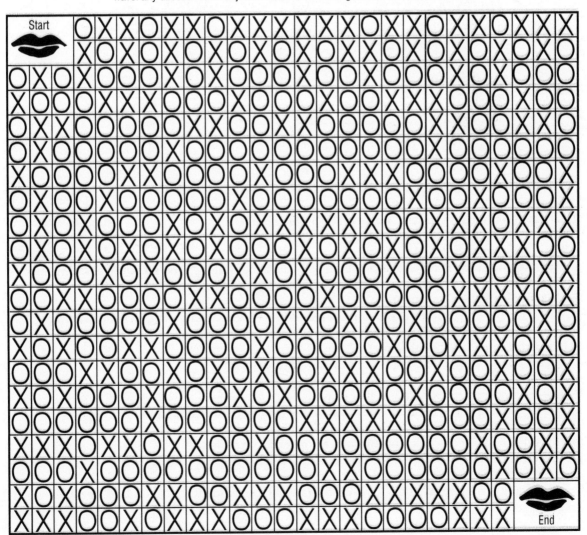

*U*nscramble the names below to reveal some of the more notorious Bible "villains"—some who waged war against God's people, others who refused to step in when the innocent were suffering. Use the clues only if you must!

RAIBMA DAN TADHNA _ _ _ _ _ _ _ _ _ _ _ _ Ⓞ _ _ _ (3 words)

HACNA _ _ _ _Ⓞ

ROHED RAGPIPA _ _ _Ⓞ_ _ _ _ _ _ _ _I (2 words)

HAAZ _ _ _ _

BEMRAJOO _ _ _ _ _ _ _ I

BUAIH DAN DBANA _ _ _ _Ⓞ_ _ _ _ _ _ _ _Ⓞ (2 words)

MOANN _ _ _ _ _

HIHTALAA _ _ _ _ _Ⓞ_ _

GEOD HET MEETIOD _ _ _ _ _ _ _ _ _ _ _ _ _Ⓞ_ (3 words)

HAPRUSH _ _ _ _ _ _ _

BATLALANS _ _ _ _Ⓞ_ _ _ _

ORMHEAOB _ _ _ _ _ _ _ _

TUSLURTEL _ _Ⓞ_ _ _ _ _ _

EAKDEZHI _ _ _ _ _Ⓞ_ _

YALSEM _ Ⓞ_ _ _ _

(Note: The clues are not in the same order as the words above.)

1. Jeremiah renamed this priest "Terror on Every Side"
2. A sorcerer also known as Bar-Jesus
3. Saul's henchman, he killed God's priests
4. The last king of Judah rebelled against the Babylonians, resulting in his recapture and Jerusalem's destruction
5. He raped his half-sister, Tamar
6. This governor of Samaria tried to stop the rebuilding of Jerusalem during Nehemiah's time
7. The first king of Israel who established a nonlevitical priesthood
8. This prosecutor called Paul "a plague"
9. These sons of Aaron offered unholy fire and were consumed
10. He imprisoned Peter
11. The earth opened and swallowed them alive
12. The only ruling queen of Judah, she killed all the male heirs she could find
13. He caused Israel's defeat at Ai because be took items forbidden for him to have
14. He added to the heavy yoke that his father, Solomon, put on Israel
15. This eleventh king of Judah sacrificed his son in worship to other gods

Now unscramble the circled letters to reveal the fate of those who inflict evil on God's people:

_ _ _ _ _ _ _ _ _ _ _ _ _

*T*his conversation put new light on the matter.

Clue: MESSIAH *is* TRUUCKN

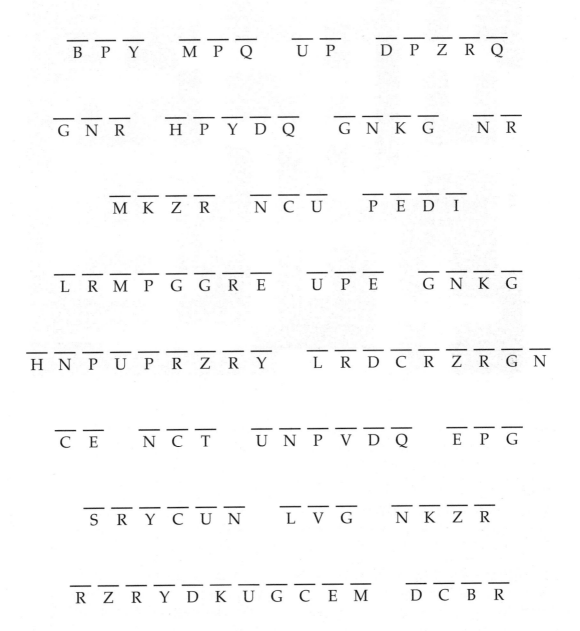

B P Y   M P Q   U P   D P Z R Q

G N R   H P Y D Q   G N K G   N R

M K Z R   N C U   P E D I

L R M P G G R E   U P E   G N K G

H N P U P R Z R Y   L R D C R Z R G N

C E   N C T   U N P V D Q   E P G

S R Y C U N   L V G   N K Z R

R Z R Y D K U G C E M   D C B R

It's easy to love the Apostle Peter. He wasn't perfect, but he tried hard. And he loved Jesus, although fear drove him to make three sorely regretted denials. The four gospels give slightly different accounts of what happened the night of Jesus' arrest.

Across

3 To restore Peter after his denial, Jesus met with him and several other apostles at the Sea of Tiberias after the resurrection and first asked Peter to "Feed My ____"

5 Later in #3 Across, Jesus asked Peter to tend and feed His ____; Peter proclaimed his love for the Lord three times, effectively "canceling" his three previous denials of Jesus

7 When Peter realized that Jesus' prediction about his denials had come true, he ____ bitterly

9 Luke says that when #19 Across crowed, Jesus turned and ____ at Peter, no doubt with sadness

12 Peter's name means this

13 Another word for #19 Across

15 In Matthew, Jesus said all His apostles would be made to ____ because of Him, leading Peter to say that he would not

18 Peter was heard to "offer epithets" when accused of knowing Jesus

19 This bird's crow came after Peter's third denial in the book of Matthew (NKJ)

21 Jesus said Peter would "refuse to admit" that he knew Him

22 Peter was willing to be incarcerated or to ____ with Jesus.

24 This high priest had once counseled the Jews that it was expedient that one man should lose his life for the people; Jesus was taken to him the night of Peter's denial

25 How many times the bird crowed in the book of Mark

27 Jesus told Peter that although the devil would attempt to sway him, He had prayed that his faith would not ____.

28 Peter was the son of John, although some translations say his name was ____.

29 It was in the ____ of Gethsemane that Peter tried to prove his devotion to Jesus, but Jesus called him off

30 This fallen angel asked for Peter, but Peter had Jesus' prayers to buoy his faith

Down

1 #30 Across wanted to sift Peter as this grain

2 One person who accused Peter of knowing Jesus said that his speech, or accent, had ____ him; he was obviously from Galilee as Jesus was

4 This servant of the high priest lost his ear to Peter's sword in Gethsemane

5 Jesus said that when they struck the ____, the sheep of the flock—His apostles—would be scattered

6 Mark says Peter went out onto the ____ of the high priest's residence after his first denial, and heard #19 Across crow

8 It was ironic that Peter said he would follow Jesus into ____or to death itself, since he was indeed locked up in one in the book of Acts

10 All right (slang)

11 John says Peter and another "apostle" followed Jesus when He was taken from Gethsemane

14 At the high priest's residence, some of the people who were with him included elders and these teachers

16 Jesus' prayer for Peter, after the denials, was that he would return to Him and strengthen his ____—followers of Jesus who would be looking to him for leadership

17 It was in this area (NKJ) adjacent to the high priest's residence that servants and officers had gathered, and that Peter was approached by people who said he had been one of Jesus' followers

20 Editor (abbr.)

23 In Matthew, Peter denied with one of these strong words that he knew Jesus

24 The Aramaic name for Peter, used in Acts

26 John says that Jesus was taken to see this man first; he was the father-in-law of the high priest

Unscramble the circled letters to find out what Peter needed—and received—after be denied Jesus.

__ __ __ __ __ V __ __ __ __ __

MIRACLE OF LIGHT

*T*he menorah candelabrum is a central part of the Jewish Hanukkah celebration commemorating one of the great victories in Jewish history, the victory of Judah the Maccabee over the Syrian-Greeks under King Antiochus IV. In the second century B.C., the Jews of Palestine were under Greek domination and prohibited from practicing their Jewish rituals. The temple was defiled with the worship of Greek gods and the sacrifice of pigs.

A revolt against the Greeks broke out, led by the priest Mattathias and carried on by his son Judah and his four brothers. They successfully freed Jerusalem from the Greek control, and they set about to purify the temple. All except one cruse of oil had been desecrated by the Greeks, but when the menorah was lit in the temple, the one cruse of oil miraculously burned for eight days — the time it took to make more oil.

During Hanukkah the eight candles of the menorah are lit — one each day of the holiday. A ninth candle, the *shamash*, is a "servant" candle which is used to light the others but is not regarded as one of the lights. Because of the tradition of lighting the candles, Hanukkah is also called the Festival of Lights.

Unscramble the words to the left to reveal what belongs ultimately to God.

RSTUT

HOPWRSI

GSETNRTH

RLYGO

NODIMION

ILEF

REGNEY

DWONKLEGE

IKONGMD

NSAEWRS

EWRRAD

GLAEALICNE

ROONH

EBOIECDNE

TNOVIEOD

TUFRUE

EASRPI

ESRROUCSE

TSJEAMY

OVLE

OHCCIE

ORWEP

RCWON

*L*ove... the greatest gift, the more excellent way.

Across
1 Forbearing
5 Juvenile (n.)
8 Anointing substance
9 Male offspring
10 Unfold
11 Very small child
12 Goes with cymbal
15 Wicked
19 . . . Now remain these ____ . . .
21 Considered, deduced
24 Profound

26 Harvest
27 Not black or white (alternate spelling)
29 Jealousy
30 Color
31 Obnoxious
32 Suspend
33 Vapor
34 Distant
36 Goes with gong
38 Rascal
40 Sick
42 Idea, consideration
43 A biblical language

44 Used to be

Down
1 Portion
2 Fact. verity
3 Simple
4 Languages
5 Group, family
6 The greatest of these
7 Relocate
13 Looking glass
14 Prediction
16 Referendum
17 Not out

18 Conducted
20 One of the three
22 Fury
23 Take joy
25 Enigmas
28 Twelve months
32 Corridor
33 Male people
34 One of the three
35 Despise
36 Bumpkin
37 Face or cup
39 Comprehend
41 Research room

Unscramble the names of the twelve people(s) below to reveal a place they all had in common.

IPILTHNSISE __ __ __ __ __ __ __ __ __ __ __

DNIEGO __ __ __ Ⓞ __ __

INAHMOA __ __ __ __ __ __ __

SHSHTHOBIE __ __ __ - __ __ __ __ Ⓞ __ __

BAHA __ __ __ __

EKALSMIATE __ __ __ Ⓞ __ __ __ __ __ __

IJLHEA Ⓞ __ __ __ __ __

BONTHA __ __ __ __ __ __

EEZEBJL __ __ Ⓞ __ __ __ __

AJORM __ __ Ⓞ __ __

EHJU Ⓞ __ __ __

IMNIADTIES __ __ __ __ __ __ __ __ __ __

Unscramble the circled letters to reveal the name of one of the Bible's most famous valleys.

__ __ __ __ __ __ __

BITTER AND SWEET

*A*fter three days walking in dusty, dry, hot sand with nothing to drink, the children of Israel weren't sure whether to believe their eyes. It looked like an oasis up ahead — or were they imagining it?

They had just narrowly escaped from the Egyptian army, but now they were beginning to wonder if it was really going to be worth it. After all, when they were slaves in Egypt they at least had the security of knowing there would be enough to eat and drink. Now there was a lot of uncertainty. Even though they knew God had promised them a nation of their own, this seemed like an unlikely way for God to treat His chosen people.

Was it too good to be true? Well, it was an oasis all right — the name was Marah — but the water was bitter and not fit to drink. That was almost too much to bear. But Moses said the Lord told him to throw a tree into the water. It seemed like a strange thing to do, but at this point it was worth a try. And do you know what? The water turned sweet, and the Israelites drank all the water they wanted. This was a story they definitely would tell their grandchildren.

Start ↓

↑ End

No doubt, this was not what anyone had in mind.

Clue: MESSIAH *is* TXLLDVU

V E B   M U X I   H X Z X   V Q Q

C D Q Q X B   H D M U   M U X

U P Q I   L O D Z D M   V E B

A X Y V E   M P   L O X V R

H D M U   P M U X Z   M P E Y G X L

V L   M U X   L O D Z D M

Y V K X   M U X T

G M M X Z V E W X

60

*D*oes being a Christian really make any difference? Paul spells it all out in Romans, in straightforward language so there's no misunderstanding. Unscramble the letters and fill in the grid and you'll see the difference—like night and day.

REEF — —|— —

TRIPSI — —|— — —

ROLGY — —|— — —

SHIRE — —|— — —

TRIBELY — — — — —|— —

FILE — — —|—

CONEDEBIE — —|— — — — — —

MINTREEQUER (NKJ) — — —|— — — — —

NOSSNADSTAREDHUG — — —|— — — — — — — — — — (3 words)

TODOPINA — — — — — —|—

APECE — —|— — —

SEJUSSHIRTC — — — — —|— — — — (2 words)

ISITFUDJE — —|— — — — —

CAUDSEC — —|— — — —

LANDMO —|— — — — — (2 words)

RACLAN — — —|— —

DEGOBAN — — —|— — —

SHELF — —|— —

NITEMY — —|— — —

INS — —|—

AWL — —|—

HATED — — —|—

LUTIG — —|— —

PINTOCUROR — — — — — — —|—

KESFEELINGS — — — — — — — —|— — (2 words)

*I*n the days of satellite communications it's almost hard to imagine what the first Christians were up against to take the Gospel to all people. The fact that by the end of the first century the Word had been spread to three continents is a tribute to (among other things) the zeal and commitment of our ancestors in the faith. Find hidden in the letter box below the names of roads in Bible times and the available means of transportation.

U	I	O	S	B	N	V	V	I	O	L	H	H	D	Y
O	W	N	J	E	R	I	C	H	O	R	O	A	D	A
S	B	I	P	S	E	A	Z	E	L	W	R	B	U	W
R	O	A	D	T	O	E	M	M	A	U	S	T	R	H
B	A	L	T	I	R	G	W	R	M	N	E	Q	T	G
S	T	O	O	F	M	N	E	R	A	O	P	H	X	I
O	P	E	B	Y	C	A	R	P	O	D	G	T	I	H
S	Y	O	N	R	R	T	P	O	E	I	U	I	T	S
M	E	R	O	S	T	I	F	L	A	A	O	P	W	G
S	K	O	G	R	A	A	O	R	T	S	V	O	Y	N
O	N	D	A	N	O	Y	T	W	L	Z	H	H	O	I
B	O	R	W	N	I	S	U	T	E	R	X	I	V	K
O	D	A	M	A	S	C	U	S	R	O	A	D	P	L
T	Y	S	J	K	W	P	T	I	X	Y	W	A	L	N

Word Pool

APPIAN WAY   BOAT   DAMASCUS ROAD   DONKEY   FOOT
HORSE   JERICHO ROAD   KINGS HIGHWAY   ROAD TO
EMMAUS   SHIP   STRAIGHT   VIA EGNATIA   WAGON

*I*t wasn't easy being the children of Israel. They had to contend with the Pharaoh who refused to let them go. Then, when they finally got out of his clutches, they had to deal with a holy God who expected them to toe the line. To help them do that, God made laws for every situation, in addition to the basis for all laws: the Ten Commandments. In this puzzle, you examine "commands": God's, Pharaoh's, and a few others'.

Across

3 For the tabernacle, God said to make fifty of these of gold, and couple the curtains together with them (NKJ)

5 God said to celebrate the Passover, and to kill a sheep or a _____ at twilight

8 God said to tell Pharaoh to let His people go, or He would send swarms of flies all over Egypt—except in this land, where His people lived

10 God told Moses to take sweet spices —_____ and onycha and galbanum—to make incense

12 If a man stole an ox and slaughtered or sold it, he had to restore this many oxen for the stolen one

15 God told Moses to say, in the hearing of Joshua, that He would utterly blot out the remembrance of these people from under Heaven (use their ancestor's name)

16 The people were told to keep the Feast of Ingathering at this time of year

17 If a man delivered an animal to his neighbor and it died, was hurt, or ran away, and no one saw it happen, an _____ (affirmation) of the Lord was put between them that indicated noninterference

19 Before coming upon Mt. Sinai, God told Moses to have the people wash these as part of the sanctification rite

20 Every man had to give a ransom for himself to the Lord when Moses took this head count (NKJ)

22 If you take a neighbor's garment as a pledge, God said, return it to him before this goes down

23 The priest of _____ told his daughters to call Moses, "that he may eat bread," after Moses helped water their flocks

26 Take no ____, God said. It blinds the discerning (no doubt with dollar signs) (NKJ)

28 The first time God told Moses to put his hand in his bosom, he drew it out and found it was ____ like snow

30 If a maidservant didn't please her master and was betrothed to him, he had no right to sell her to this type of people, because he had dealt deceitfully with her (NKJ)

31 That is (abbr.)

32 To hallow Aaron and his sons as priests, Moses had to feed them unleavened ____ anointed with oil, made of wheat flour

33 If a servant refused to leave his master in the seventh year, the year of freedom, his master was to pierce his ear with this, and the servant would then serve him forever (NKJ)

36 White ____ snow

38 Aaron and his sons had to wash their hands and feet in a ____ made of bronze (NKJ)

39 To amplify #6 Down, God said He would cut off the Amorites, Hittites, Perizzites, Canaanites, ____, and Jebusites

41 Don't let her live, God said of a woman who practiced magic (NKJ)

45 I. . . you. . . he. . . she. . . ____

46 A "man of no means" could not be shown partiality in his dispute

47 Pharaoh told Moses to "plead his case" with God after the flies came

48 God said to tell the people not to touch this part of Mt. Sinai

49 God told Moses he could return to Egypt, because the men who had sought his life were ____.

51 God told Moses to leave Mt. Sinai and warn the people, lest they break through the bounds to gaze at the Lord and meet this fate

52 God said to celebrate the Feast of Unleavened Bread, to remember when God brought the Israelite "troops" out of Egypt

53 If a man acted with premeditation against his neighbor, and killed him with "craftiness," death was his sentence

Down

1 God said to carve six of these on each of the two onyx stones, for the twelve tribes

2 Meat that had been torn by beasts in the field had to be thrown to these animals, and not eaten by the people

4 After obeying God's command, Moses saw the waters of Egypt turn to blood; the fish died and the river "smelled bad"

5 If a thief was struck and killed when caught breaking in, there was to be no "remorse" for his bloodshed

6 If they did all that God spoke to them, the people could count on God's being one of these to their enemies

7 If a fire broke out and caught in "a rose's chief drawback," so that grain or a field was consumed, the kindler had to make restitution

9 After setting the altar of gold for the incense before the #27 Down, Moses had to put up the "partition" for the door of the tabernacle (NKJ)

10 God told Moses to tell the people to ask their Egyptian neighbors for articles made of this shiny material

11 Obey My voice and keep My covenant, God said, and you (the Israelites) will be "a special ____" to Me, something of value (NKJ)

13 If an ox tended to thrust with this in times past, and the owner knew it, and the ox killed someone, the ox and his owner had to be put to death

14 God said He would rescue the Israelites from ____, redeem them with an outstretched arm (NKJ)

18 On a plate of pure gold, the artisans were told to engrave "____ TO THE LORD"

19 God told Moses to say that He would send severe pestilence on all Egyptian livestock: cattle, horses, donkeys, ____, oxen, and sheep

21 A man who stole a sheep had to restore this many sheep for the stolen one

24 Don't "trouble" the widow or the fatherless child, God said

25 After setting up the tabernacle of the tent of meeting, Moses had to put the #27 Down in it and partition that that off with a __ (NKJ)

26 The boils in #37 Down broke out on man and__

27 God said to make this "container" for His Testimony of acacia wood

29 The people were to overthrow their enemies and completely break down their sacred "obelisks"

32 When eating the Passover meal, God said, wear a belt on this (NKJ)

33 On the lampstand's branches, God said to make three bowls like this "nut" blossom on each branch

34 If you make an altar of stone, God said, don't use hewn stone; that would ____ it (NKJ)

35 God told Moses to lift his rod over the Red Sea, causing it to ____

37 God told Moses and Aaron to take handfuls of these from a furnace and scatter them toward Heaven; they'd cause boils

40 God said to make altars of this "dirt"

42 God told Moses to stretch out his hand over the waters of Egypt: streams, ____, ponds, and pools

43 God said to tell all gifted artisans to make Aaron's garments: breastplate, ephod, robe, tunic, turban, and ____ (NKJ)

44 According to orders, the artisans left an opening for this in the middle of Aaron's robe (NKJ)

48 When preparing the Passover lamb, God said, don't do this to its bones

50 God told Moses to strike this with his rod so it would become lice

The Bible is full of good advice on how to conduct our lives. It tells us what to think about, what to do, how to treat others—and most important of all, how to relate to God our Father. This puzzle, a verse from the Old Testament book that's known for dispensing sage counsel, addresses the whole issue of how to use our heads.

(Note: The words of the verse have been scrambled.)

Clue: MESSIAH *is* 3 17 24 24 19 1 23

19 4   21 17 1 20   13 8

7 8 20 13   5 17   8 14 4

4 8 26   6 8 22 20   26 23 17

13 17 12 1 20 26   14 19 24 17

17 18 19 7   17 6 17 24

1 4 13   21 20 8 3

Unscramble the words:

Connect adjacent letters (in all directions) to discover how to experience enduring power. (Note: the first and last letters of the message are the same.)

A   K   L   A   W   L   L   A   H   S   Y   E   H

N   H   E   L   L   A   T   H   E   I   S   T   T

D   N   T   O   L   H   W   E   T   R   E   R   D

N   O   R   D   S   R   E   N   H   G   N   E   N

O   P   U   T   Y   E   H   T   L   G   A   S   A

T   A   T   W   I   S   S   E   H   A   L   A   Y

F   H   Y   A   A   H   T   S   U   R   L   S   R

A   T   H—E   L   L   H   Y   N   A   G   O   A

I   Ⓣ   U   O   M   W   E   H   N   N   T   E

N   N   T   U   P   I   T   W   I   D   B   E   W

*T*his puzzle should be "E-sy." It's all about people, places, and things in the Bible that start with the letter "E." (We've also thrown in some adjectives and verbs that have special meaning.)

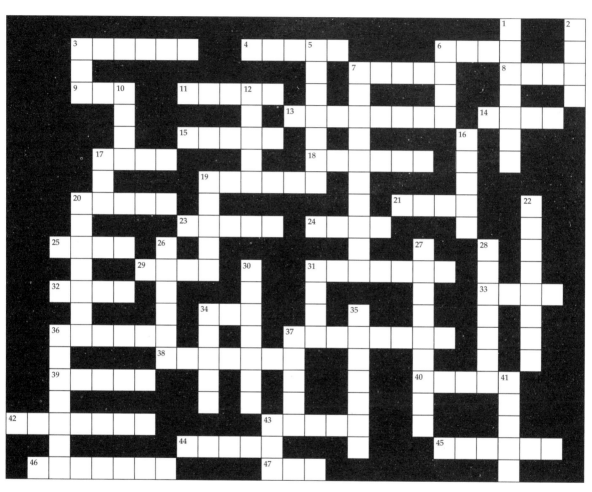

Across

3 He wanted a double portion of his mentor's spirit

4 Younger people, submit to the _____ person, Peter said

6 But deliver us from _____

7 This king of Moab defeated Israel

8 The priest who led the exiled back to Jerusalem

9 An animal commonly used in sacrifices

11 The Israelites battled King Og of Bashan at this place

13 A time to _____, and a time to refrain from this (third-person sing.)

14 A town in southern Judah that probably belonged to both Judah and Simeon (NKJ)

15 Great-grandfather of Samuel

17 It was perfect, except for the snake

18 "Strongly tell" servants to be obedient to their masters, Paul told Titus

19 On the road to this village, Jesus met two followers after His resurrection

20 The Israelites finally got out of here

21 Rachel to Jacob: "Give me children, or 'otherwise' I die!"

23 A priestly garment

24 Saul and his men encamped in this valley—and met Goliath

25 This left-handed Benjaminite stabbed and killed the king of Moab

29 Wrath kills a foolish man, and this slays a simple one

31 In Heaven, John said, the rainbow around the throne appeared like this gem

32 He put his stomach before his birthright

33 The father-in-law of #32 Across

34 Told that the ark had been captured, this high priest fell, broke his neck, and died

36 She replaced Queen Vashti

37 "God is with us"

38 A fellow worker with Paul

39 A son of Cain

40 In Psalms, God renews your youth like the bird's

42 Pharaoh Neco changed this king's name to Jeholakim

43 This Philistine city met God's wrath in Amos

44 The men of Dedan brought Tyre ivory tusks and this durable wood as payment

45 It took forty days to properly do this to the body of someone who had died

46 Samuel's father

47 Nehemiah prayed ". . . let Your ____ be attentive and Your eyes open"

3 She was first

5 Christ must reign until He puts all these under His feet

6 Son of Seth (Greek spelling)

7 The seventh angel in Revelation poured out his bowl, and this is what happened

10 His son, Gaal, fought against Abimelech

12 An encampment during the Exodus

16 A city in Judah (also a common anesthetic, in our century)

17 Is there taste in the white of this? Job asked

19 Jesus' tomb was ____ on the first day of the week

20 One of the seven churches in Revelation

22 The land south of #20 Across

26 Weeping may "last" for a night, but joy comes in the morning

27 Naomi's husband

28 Forever

30 A letter

31 Another name for #32 Across

34 "I will ____ You, I will praise Your name," said Isaiah (NKJ)

35 Like an ____ of gold is a wise reprover to one who listens and obeys

36 God made him a watchman for the house of Israel

37 A descendant of King Saul, and brother of Azel

41 A dry measure that's a little over a U.S. bushel

43 ____ for an ____

Down

1 A son of Aaron

2 Joshua built an altar to the Lord in Mount ____, to renew the covenant

If you found the crossword puzzle "e-sy," you'll want to find out what the Bible says is easy. The letter "e"—and all the other vowels, including "y"—have been taken out of this verse. Add the vowels where they are needed to complete the words in this Scripture.

FRMKSSNDMBRDNSLGHT.

*T*ry to solve the equation below, based on the ages of people in the Bible, without consulting the references!

The age of Enoch when he "walked with God" (Gen 5:23-24)   _____

The age of Lamech when his son Noah was born (Gen 5:28)   +   _____

The maximum age of the children Herod ordered to be killed in
Bethlehem (Matt 2:16)   ×   _____

The age of Noah when the rains began to fall (Gen 7:11)   —   _____

The age of Methusaleh when he died (Gen 5:27)   +   _____

The age of Abram when he departed out of Haran with Sarai
and Lot (Gen 12:4)   —   _____

The age of Adam when his son Seth was born (Gen 5:3)   +   _____

The minimum age of males counted in the giving of portions by
Hezekiah (2 Chron 31:16)   ÷   _____

The age of Jared when his son Enoch was born (Gen 5:18)   +   _____

The age of Seth when his son Enos was born (Gen 5:6)   +   _____

The age of Cainan when his son Mahalaleel was born (Gen 5:12)   +   _____

The age at which Levites began to have a course of service
under Hezekiah (2 Chron 31:17)   —   _____

The age of King Jehoiada when he died (2 Chron 24:15)   +   _____

The age of Joseph when he became second in command to
Pharaoh (Gen 41:46)   —   _____

The age of Enoch when his son Methuselah was born (Gen 5:21)   +   _____

The age of Jesus when he went to Jerusalem for Passover and
"tarried behind" in the Temple (Luke 2:42)   +   _____

The number of years that are as a day in the Lord's sight
(Ps 90:4)   =   _____

Unscramble the twelve words below, which are all associated with one of the most evil people in Israel's history.

TAEHBLA __ __ __ Ⓞ __ __ __

OPREPTHS __ __ __ __ __ __ __ __

EUQNE __ __ __ Ⓞ __

ISADINON (NKJ) __ __ __ __ __ __ __ __ __

NOTBAH __ __ __ __ __ __

CUNHUES Ⓞ __ __ __ __ __ __

IEJHLA Ⓞ __ __ __ __ __

SGDO __ __ __ __

EERLJEZ __ __ Ⓞ __ __ __ Ⓞ

YVNAEIDR __ __ __ __ __ __ __ __

UJEH Ⓞ __ __ __

BAAH __ __ __ __

Unscramble the circled letters to reveal the name that has become so closely associated with the word "wicked":

__ __ __ __ __ __ __

The names of the New Testament books will complete this crossword.

Across

1 The Lord's return
5 Letter to seven churches
6 Christ is supreme
8 The King's Gospel
10 I am the Son of God
12 True religion
13 The Church is born
15 Glory of the Church
16 Paul's thank-you letter
17 Fullness in Christ

Down

1 Paul's last word
2 Written to Theophilus, a Gentile Christian
3 The Servant of the Lord
4 Church problems
7 The Gospel manifesto
9 Letter to church leader in Crete
10 Contend for the faith
11 Do Gentiles have to become Jews to become
   Christian?
14 Slaves and brothers
16 Hope in suffering

In the Old Testament and the New, God was there for the people in their present; but He wanted them to know that He would be in their future as well. He used prophets to tell the people some of what they could expect in the years—and centuries—and eternity—to come. As we read the prophets, we see some precious promises, and we see them fulfilled before the Bible's last page was written. The verse below is just one of those promises—good news for everyone. (Note: The words are scrambled.)

Clue: MESSIAH *is* 15 2 20 20 3 1 11

16 1 15 2   7 4 5 16 20 2 14 4 19

2 22 2 19 14 1 20 21 3 16 10   23 3 14 14

3 20   1 16 8   9 4 19   5 20   4 9

7 11 3 14 8   10 4 22 2 19 16 15 2 16 21

5 16 21 4   1   17 19 3 16 7 2

20 11 4 5 14 8 2 19   20 4 16   10 4 8   5 20

11 3 20   3 20   17 2 1 7 2   1   10 3 22 2 16

5 17 4 16   1 16 8   5 16 21 4   6 4 19 16

7 1 14 14 2 8   15 3 10 11 21 25   6 2   11 3 20

23 4 16 8 2 19 9 5 14   21 11 2

23 3 14 14   6 2   9 1 21 11 2 19.

Unscramble the words: _____

Find the names of the eight men who linked Adam to Noah in the box of letters below.

E	M	B	W	S	L	T	N	L	A	M	E
N	A	E	N	I	A	J	U	H	T	E	M
S	J	H	T	A	C	A	S	H	A	M	J
O	A	M	E	H	D	R	E	O	A	H	A
C	J	A	I	N	U	E	L	I	N	E	L
L	A	M	E	C	H	S	A	H	C	E	R
E	R	N	A	L	C	R	E	A	E	P	U
T	E	S	H	M	A	E	H	L	S	N	E
H	D	P	C	N	I	D	A	I	A	O	S
E	A	R	A	E	N	L	E	H	U	H	E
D	I	D	M	J	A	M	N	E	T	T	L
A	N	A	S	H	N	H	C	O	N	E	A
C	E	L	A	H	A	M	O	D	E	S	H
A	N	M	I	A	C	U	I	R	A	J	I

Unscramble the names of these ten Bible figures, who shared a common experience.

OSSME __ __ O __ __

ALNAB __ __ __ __ __

ASMHE __ O __ O __

AVDDI __ __ __ __ O

AJZZI __ __ __ __ __

EBLA __ __ O __

JBOCA __ __ __ __ __

ORLD __ __ O __

EOHJSP __ __ __ __ OO

BAHAMRA __ __ __ __ __ __ __

Unscramble the circled letters to reveal the profession associated with them all:

__ __ __ __ __ __ __ __

*P*aul's high-sea adventure on his way to Italy for trial is one of the most dramatic stories in the New Testament. Most of the clues and answers relate to that famous journey.

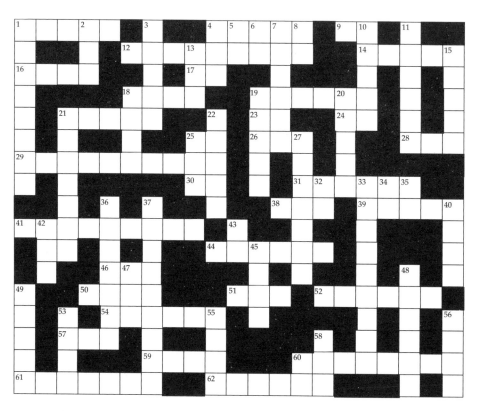

Across

1 A welcome sight to the crew and passengers on board the ill-fated Alexandrian sailing vessel
4 To act for another's benefit
9 You and me
12 Cornelius was a _____ of the Italian army
14 When Paul prayed and put these on the sick, they got well
16 Destination
17 Not off
18 Bow of a ship
19 Roman emperor
21 Grain

23 Agriculture (abbr.)
24 Northeast (abbr.)
25 Enlisted army man (abbr.)
26 Representative (abbr.)
28 _____ aground
29 "Northeaster"
30 Doctor of Divinity (abbr.)
31 Related to
38 Not healthy
39 Venomous creature
41 Perilous
44 Mediterranean island
46 Penitentiary (abbr.)
50 Lifeless

51 Inlet of the sea
52 Wrecked
54 Used for kindling
57 Inclined
59 Larger inlet
60 Hospitality
61 Unit of measurement; one is the length of arms outstretched
62 Get away

Down

 1 Killer
 2 Fasten
 3 Be encouraged; take _____
 4 While the storm raged, this was not seen
 5 Emergency room (abbr.)
 6 Rhode Island (abbr.)
 7 Nautical journey
 8 Half an em-space
10 Beach
11 Mainstay
13 Pull
15 Rear end of a boat
18 He had been through it all—shipwrecked, beaten, imprisoned, stoned
19 Freight
20 God's messenger
21 Paul's was ignored

22 These were contrary, causing threatening sailing conditions
25 The island natives thought Paul was one of these because he seemed immune to poison
27 Chief official of #1 Across
32 Elevated (abbr.)
33 To lighten the ship so it could sail faster and farther, its contents were thrown here
34 Nickel (abbr.)
35 General practitioner (abbr.)
36 Violent storm
37 To measure depth, take _____
40 This fell on the already soaked crew and passengers
42 How many people would be saved from drowning in the shipwreck
43 Near
45 Implore deity
47 Paul encouraged the people on board to do this to survive
48 Made well
49 Light rowboat
53 What one does on the Day of Atonement
55 Not threatened
56 Paul predicted this if they sailed
58 Those aboard the ship had given up hope and expected to _____
60 Kitchen patrol (abbr.)

The Apostle Paul went through great hardships for the Gospel, and, according to tradition, he made the ultimate sacrifice—martyrdom—for his faith. How did Paul regard his suffering? The well-known verse below tells us. To find out, put the words in their proper sequence.

TO BE WORTHY THIS BE WHICH ARE IN TIME I THE NOT REVEALED SUFFERINGS THAT WITH GLORY FOR PRESENT OF CONSIDER THE COMPARED SHALL

_____

_____

_____

PETER'S PRISON RELEASE

*A*fter Herod killed James, the brother of John, and saw that it pleased the Jewish leaders, he arrested Peter and put him under the guard of four squads of soldiers. While Peter was sleeping, chained between two soldiers, an angel smote him on the side and ordered him to get up and put on his sandals in preparation for leaving the prison. As Peter arose, the chains fell off his wrists.

The angel then proceeded to lead Peter out of the prison past the first and second guard posts and out the iron gate (which swung open of its own accord) that led to the city. (See Acts 12:10.) After the angel had led Peter down a street, the angel disappeared from Peter's sight. Until that moment, Peter had thought that he was experiencing a vision. After the angel departed, the Bible tells that Peter "came to himself" and realized he had been delivered by the Lord. He immediately made his way to a house where Christians were in prayer for his release.

Find the route the angel took to free Peter. Note: The prison guards can guard a pathway in all four directions.

*T*ake a word of advice from our old friend Solomon: Read Proverbs and rediscover wisdom! Fill in the missing words, match up the two halves of each proverb, and unscramble the circled letters to describe "the right word at the right time."

1. Do not enter the path of the

__ __ __ __ __ Ⓞ .

A. But a foolish son is the

Ⓞ __ __ __ __ of his mother.

2. Honor the Lord with your

Ⓞ __ __ __ __ __ __ __ __ __

B. But love __ Ⓞ __ __ __ __ all

sins.

3. Evil Ⓞ __ __ __ __ __ __ __

sinners,

C. And do not walk in the way of

Ⓞ __ __ Ⓞ .

4. A wise son makes a __ Ⓞ __ __

father,

D. But to the righteous __ __ Ⓞ __

shall be repaid.

5. __ Ⓞ __ __ __ __ stirs up strife,

E. And with the

__ __ __ Ⓞ_Ⓞ __ __ __ __

of all your increase.

Unscramble letters:

__ __ __ __ __ __ __   __ __   __ __ __ __

THE CELTIC CROSS

*T*his cross design is also called the Ionic Cross or Irish Cross. It is one of the most familiar forms of the cross, as well as one of the most ancient. It is widely used on church roofs and towers.

The primitive Celtic Christians trace their origin to a very early era. A number of these crosses are found in Great Britain and Ireland where they were first erected as cemetery and wayside crosses. Some of them are elaborately carved.

The circle that appears on the cross is a symbol of both eternity and wholeness. This cross design is therefore also called the Cross of Redemption.

Start ↘

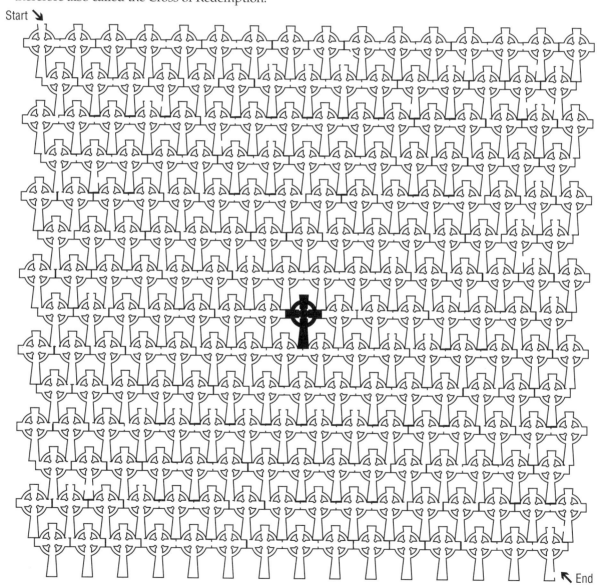

End ↖

Fill in the blanks to create a profile of the One we love.

*W*ho hath believed our report? And to whom is the ____ (9) of the LORD revealed? For he shall grow up before him as a ____ ____ (13). And as a ____ (11) out of dry ground . . . there is ____ ____ (5) that we should desire him. . . . He is ____ (6) and ____ (14) of men: a man of ____ (1). And acquainted with ____ (16): . . . We did esteem him ____ (8), ____ (4) of God, and ____ (17) . . . he was ____ (12) for our transgressions, he was ____ (7) for our iniquities, the ____ (10) of our peace was upon him; and with his ____ (3) we are healed . . . The Lord hath laid on him the ____ (19) of us all. . . . He was ____ (18), and he was afflicted . . . as a ____ (15) before her shearers is dumb, so he openeth not his mouth. . . . For he was ____ ____ (2) out of the land of the living: for the transgression of my people was he stricken. (Isaiah 53:1-8)

1   — — — — — — —

2   — — — — — —

3   — — — — — — —

4   — — — — — — —

5   — — — — — — — — (2 words)

6   — — — — — — — —

7   — — — — — — —

8   — — — — — — — —

9   — — —

10   — — — — — — — — — — —

11   — — — —

12   — — — — — — —

13   — — — — — — — — — — — (2 words)

14   — — — — — — — —

15   — — — — —

16   — — — — —

17   — — — — — — — —

18   — — — — — — — —

19   — — — — — — —

When it comes to animals mentioned in the Bible, our best friend doesn't fare too well.

Across

1 Second Peter says this type of teacher fulfilled the proverb: A dog returns to its own vomit

4 This future king of Syria thought Elisha's prophecy made him sound like a dog

5 David's enemies, like a dog, would search for food and "wail" if they weren't satisfied (NKJ)

8 Gideon's 300 were chosen to fight these people because they (the 300) lapped from the water like a dog

10 Preposition

11 "Look out for" dogs and evil workers, says Philippians

15 Israel's leaders were like "money-grubbing" dogs, never having enough, says Isaiah

17 When this king's blood was washed out of his chariot, the dogs licked it up

19 Don't give what is "sacred" to dogs

20 This beggar sat by a rich man's gate while dogs licked his sores

21 These "killers" will be kept outside the New Jerusalem, along with dogs, sorcerers, the sexually immoral, idolators, and liars (sing.)

Down

1 As a dog returns to his vomit, this type of person returns to his folly

2 God brought David's enemies back from the depths of this "water" so his dogs could have their portion

3 Not a dog moved this "lapper" against the Israelites when God took the Egyptians' firstborn

4 When Shimei cursed David, Abishai called him a dead dog and asked to remove this from his body

6 David asked whom Saul was pursuing—a dead dog? This insect found on dogs?

7 A living dog is better than this dead animal, because he has hope

8 Holy men had to throw this beast-torn "flesh" to the dogs (NKJ)

9 Was Goliath a dog, that David came to him with ____?

11 Jehu said the dogs would eat whoever belonged to this king of Israel

12 Meddling in another's quarrel is like taking a dog by these "muff holders"

13 The dogs ate this queen by the wall of Jezreel

14 The dogs also ate whoever belonged to this king of Israel; his son Nadab succeeded him

16 A woman from this region wanted the crumbs from the Lord's table, because even dogs got those

18 Bringing the price of a dog to the "abode" of the Lord for any vowed offering was an abomination

*T*his puzzle is taken from the Gospels and Acts. The phrase that you are looking for is a "command" that all Christians should follow, with great joy. To make this a little more difficult, we have added 3 letters to each scrambled word. Once you've eliminated the unnecessary letters and unscrambled each word, you can then unscramble the circled letters and find the phrase. And when you're done, it should be obvious what the 13 words have in common. (Hint: The phrase has three words.)

APIEPIHTL ◯ _ _ _ ◯ _

NATEOMSI ◯ _ _ _ _

SIMTEJAO _ ◯ _ _ _

DEATHIDHGUSA _ _ _ _ _ _ ◯ _ _

SAIJNUDG _ _ _ _ ◯

CMOSTHAIR _ _ _ ◯ _ _

JOINHER _ _ _ _

EASTJUME _ ◯ _ _ _

TREEPOST _ _ _ _ ◯

DRAWERNET _ ◯ _ _ _ _

WARMTHIENT _ _ _ _ ◯ _ _

BALTIMOREHDOWN _ _ _ _ _ _ _ _ _ ◯ _

MIANEATDHTS _ _ _ _ _ ◯ _ _

Unscramble letters:

_ _ _ _ _ _   _ _ _   _ _ _ _

*T*hroughout the Bible, significant events happened at all hours.

Across

3 Daytime, He taught in the Temple; at night He stayed on this mountain, says Luke (NKJ)

6 The bird that fed Elijah day and night

8 He received an olive leaf from a dove one night

10 Jesus was delivered to him in the morning by elders and chief priests

11 These animals pursue their prey at night, says the psalmist

13 Mister (abbr.)

14 He visited Jesus one night and identified Him as "a teacher come from God"

17 Some of the disciples couldn't catch one of these on the morning Peter swam to shore to meet the risen Lord

18 This animal was part of the burnt offering prepared every morning, per God's orders in Ezekiel

20 This member of royalty had to appoint a portion of his possessions for morning and evening burnt offerings

21 A man who rules in the fear of God is like a morning without these

24 The psalmist declared God's loving kindness morning and night with this stringed instrument

25 The torment will go on day and night for this kind of prophet

26 Jesus could return at the early A.M. crowing of this bird

Down

1 David left his woolly charges with a keeper on the morning of the day he met Goliath

2 After Joshua's 5,000 men ambushed this city, Joshua hanged its king on a tree until evening

4 A landowner hired laborers to work in this early one morning

5 The Levites stood, morning and evening, to "offer appreciation to" the Lord

7 He had a vision one night that led him to go to Macedonia

9 Second Peter says to heed the prophetic word, as a light does this in a dark place, until the day dawns

12 The day and night are God's, said Asaph; He prepared this "sky light"

13 The princes of this country stayed with Balaam one night

15 "Prayerfully ponder" God's Word, as the psalmist does during night watches

16 David would "melodiously vocalize" God's mercy in the morning .

19 When Moses did this day and night—without a jury—Jethro suggested he get help

22 Jesus is the Bright and Morning ____

23 Put on this "coat" of light, said Paul; the day is at hand

PASS THE PLATE

One of the instructions Moses received from God when he was on Mt. Sinai was to take up an offering to build a tabernacle as a dwelling place for the Lord. The tabernacle would be a portable sanctuary that would go with the people through the wilderness, a place where the Lord could be among the people of Israel on their journey to the promised land. God gave Moses exact specifications for the construction of the tabernacle and its furnishings and for making the sacred garments for the priests.

Moses told the people the Lord commanded an offering for the tabernacle from "whoever is of a willing heart." The Israelites brought earrings, nose rings, rings and necklaces, jewelry, thread, fine linen, goats' hair, red rams' skins, badger skins, acacia wood, yarn, onyx stones, spices, and oil. They brought so many offerings that the Bible says, "the people were restrained from bringing, for the material they had was sufficient for all the work to be done — indeed too much" (Exodus 36:6–7).

Pass through each item of offering before bringing it to Moses.
Do not cross back over a path that you have already used.

◆ = Offering

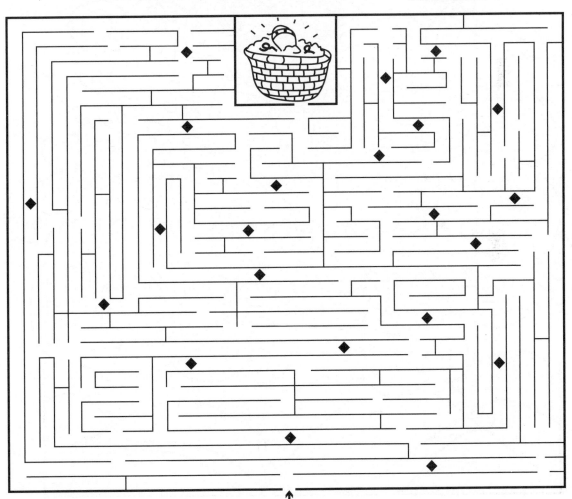

MOSES' MOUNTAINTOP EXPERIENCE

*T*he phrase "mountaintop experience" could have been coined by Moses, for indeed it was there that he saw the glory of the Lord. God told Moses to meet Him on top of Mt. Sinai. The invitation was extended to Moses, his brother Aaron, his nephews Abihu and Nadab, and seventy elders. Everyone else would worship from a distance, but only Moses was allowed to come near to God.

For six days a cloud covered the mountaintop. On the seventh day Moses saw the glory of the Lord which "was like a consuming fire." For the next forty days and nights, Moses was on the mountaintop while God gave him detailed instructions for offerings, tabernacle, furnishings, sacred garments for the priests, altars, sacrifices, and incense. And then before Moses left, God handed him two tablets of stone with the Law for the people to observe.

Mountaintop experiences are where we meet the Lord to be equipped for the business of living daily on the plain or in the valley. And that is what Moses was about to find out.

Unscramble the words on the left that are among God's provisions for us. The circled phrase reveals our appropriate response to Him!

TAEWR   — — — —

ICHLTONG   — — — — — — — —

HAIFT   — — — — —

AEDILVENREC   — — — — — — — — — —

EKDNLOWGE   — — — — — — — — —

HESETLR   — — — — — — —

SIGERVOFNES   — — — — — — — — — —

TNHISGI   — — — — — — —

IYVRCOT   — — — — — — —

DSWIMO   — — — — — —

RIFNEDIHSP   — — — — — — — — — —

AIUNGDCE   — — — — — — — —

AENHGLI   — — — — — — —

ETSRGNHT   — — — — — — — —

OFOD   — — — —

PLUPSY   — — — — — —

DERRWAS   — — — — — — —

IALSAVTNO   — — — — — — — — —

TAIRIPOSNIN   — — — — — — — — — — —

ECENSRPE   — — — — — — — —

TCPTREOOIN   — — — — — — — — — —

How do you keep those spiritual muscles from going soft?

Across

1 If we hang on and do the will of God, we'll receive this

3 Paul pressed on for the reward of the ____ ____ of God (2 words)

5 Once you've put your hand to this, don't look back to see who's gaining

7 Paul didn't just beat the air

8 An objective

11 We all run in this

13 If they're feeble, strengthen them

14 When Jesus comes, we'll receive headpieces of ____

15 Paul disciplined this

16 We don't have to run, if we do this in the light

18 Hanging on

19 If your calling is sure, you won't "trip"

21 They need straight paths

22 The race isn't to the "fast"

Down

1 Part of the race: "proclaim" the kingdom of God

2 If the Philippians were blameless, Paul hadn't run or ____ in vain

4 The reward

6 Don't become "tired" or discouraged in your souls

9 The end of our faith—the ____ of our souls

10 At the end, there will be an "opening" into the kingdom for us

12 Is yours imperishable?

17 Pursue this with all, and holiness, too

20 Our path is Jesus: The Way, the ____, and the Life

*I*n the letter box below circle the names of occupations of Bible times.

```
O   W   R   O   T   C   E   L   L   O   C   X   A   T
A   U   O   X   B   N   W   P   D   J   N   L   F   N
M   W   S   D   R   E   H   P   E   H   S   R   I   A
B   A   K   E   R   N   E   J   O   U   R   A   S   H
A   O   W   N   E   O   N   R   U   E   X   O   H   C
S   O   M   E   L   R   G   L   N   D   O   W   E   R
S   B   U   T   L   E   R   N   O   U   G   A   R   E
A   X   S   O   U   R   A   P   L   M   N   E   M   M
D   O   I   R   F   T   V   S   E   T   L   O   A   Z
O   R   C   S   E   N   E   O   I   L   O   Q   N   E
R   O   I   E   M   B   R   O   I   D   E   R   E   R
S   C   A   R   P   E   N   T   E   R   O   W   J   Z
O   U   N   R   R   O   T   A   R   O   P   Z   L   A
```

Word Pool

AMBASSADOR   BAKER   BUTLER   CARPENTER   EMBROIDERER
ENGRAVER   FISHERMAN   FULLER   JUDGE   MERCHANT   MUSICIAN
ORATOR   SHEPHERD   TANNER   TAX COLLECTOR   TILLER

God asked the Israelites to make a place for Him where He could be in their midst. They followed His instructions to the letter, and when He was there, it was obvious.

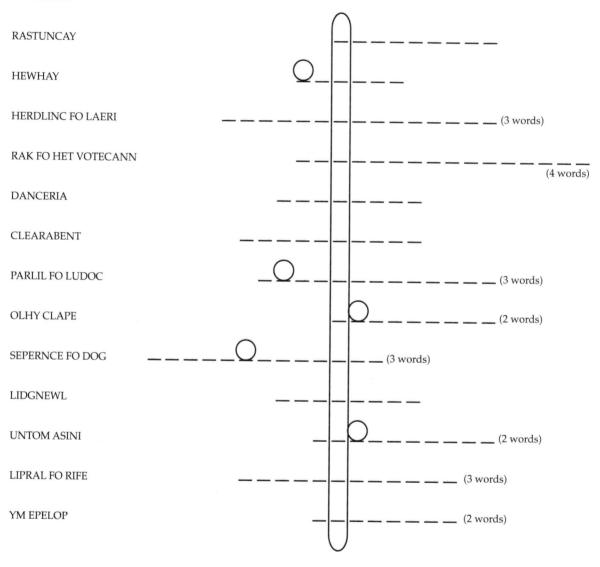

RASTUNCAY

HEWHAY

HERDLINC FO LAERI — (3 words)

RAK FO HET VOTECANN — (4 words)

DANCERIA

CLEARABENT

PARLIL FO LUDOC — (3 words)

OLHY CLAPE — (2 words)

SEPERNCE FO DOG — (3 words)

LIDGNEWL

UNTOM ASINI — (2 words)

LIPRAL FO RIFE — (3 words)

YM EPELOP — (2 words)

Unscramble the circled letters to reveal where God dwells now:

— —   — — —

(See 1 Corinthians 3:16.)

The longest prayer of Jesus recorded in Scripture is one He prayed for Himself, His disciples, and for all those who would come to believe in Him. He prayed this prayer on the night He was betrayed. Some of His last concerns and requests on our behalf are found in this prayer in John 17. Most of the clues below are from that chapter.

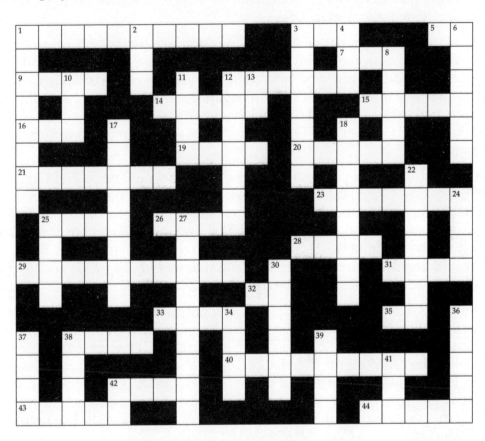

Across
1 Creation
3 Deity
5 In the world, but not ____ it
7 Is (pl.)
9 Designation
12 See
14 Granted
15 Actual fact
16 Male offspring
19 Sinister
20 Humanity
21 Never ending
23 Flawless
25 History
26 World's attitude toward Christians
28 God's attitude toward people
29 Made known
31 Remove
32 Not you
33 Task
35 You and I; in this instance, Father and Son
38 Sacred
40 Destruction
42 Go forth
43 Global perspective, ____-view

44 Savior

Down
1 Completed
2 Everyone
3 Bring honor
4 In Greek, "Abba"
6 Male parent
8 Inhabited plane
10 Jesus' 12 disciples were these
11 #21 Across ____, is to know God and His Son
12 To accept in faith
13 Half an em-space
17 Set apart

18 Accepted
22 Proclaim
24 Not false
25 When you speak to God
27 Power
30 Want
34 To be faithful to
36 God spoke these
37 Understand
38 Time
39 Jesus prayed that those God gave Him could be ____Him
41 United
42 Special delivery (abbr.)

RUN FOR YOUR LIFE

*J*ezebel should have left well enough alone. When she came up against the prophet Elijah she had more than met her match. She didn't realize that her 450 priests of Baal and 400 prophets of Asherah were no contest for Elijah's God, the God of Abraham, Isaac, and Jacob.

Jezebel's marriage to Ahab was arranged for political reasons, and when she moved to Israel she brought with her the worship of foreign gods. The influence of paganism spread in Israel and corrupted the worship of the Israelite God. Ahab did nothing to stop the increasing paganism. In fact, King Ahab "did more to provoke the LORD God of Israel to anger than all the kings of Israel who were before him" (1 Kings 16:33). Critics of Jezebel's foreign gods were executed or avenged.

Elijah spoke the word of the Lord to Ahab that there would be drought in Israel. After three years, God told Elijah to tell Ahab that He would send rain on the earth. This was Elijah's opportunity for a test of strength between the pagan fertility gods and the God of Israel. "If the LORD is God, follow Him; but if Baal, follow him," he declared (18:21). The rules of the contest were simple: Both sides would prepare a bull for sacrifice. Each side would call on his god, and the god who answered by fire would be declared the true God.

The contest took place on Mount Carmel. The prophets of Baal invoked their god until evening to send fire, but in the end "no one answered" (v. 26). Elijah prepared his altar and sacrifice, then had his men drench it with water three times. When he called on the "LORD God of Abraham, Isaac, and Israel," the "fire of the LORD fell and consumed the burnt sacrifice, and the wood and the stones and the dust, and it licked up the water that was in the trench. Now when all the people saw it, they fell on their faces; and they said, 'The LORD, He is God! The LORD, He is God!'" (18:36–39).

In short time, a cloudburst came and ended the drought. A clear and decisive victory was won by Elijah's God. To bring an end to the pagan worship, Elijah put to death the prophets of Baal. When word reached Jezebel of the execution, she threatened the prophet with his life. "When he saw that, he arose and ran for his life, and went to Beersheba" (19:3).

Elijah's life has been threatened, and he needs to get out of sight in a big hurry. Help him escape to Beersheba through this maze without being seen by Jezebel's cohorts.

Your destiny is awesome.

Clue: MESSIAH *is* QIGGMET

F Y H   K I   E P P '   K M H T

Y R Z I M P I X   J E W I '

F I T C P X M R S   E G   M R   E

Q M V V C V   H T I   S P C V A   C J

H T I   P C V X '   E V I   F I M R S

H V E R G J C V Q I X   M R H C   H T I

G E Q I   M Q E S I   J V C Q

S P C V A   H C   S P C V A .

The words of the song most commonly called "The Doxology" are used to complete this crossword grid. We've given you a word as a starting point. Fit in the rest of the words as quickly as you can. (Can you complete the puzzle in under five minutes?)

Praise God, from whom all blessings flow;
Praise Him, all creatures here below;
Praise Him above, ye heav'nly host;
Praise Father, Son and Holy Ghost.

Puzzle Answers

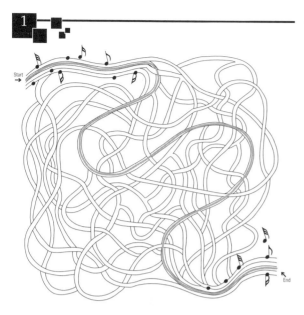

1

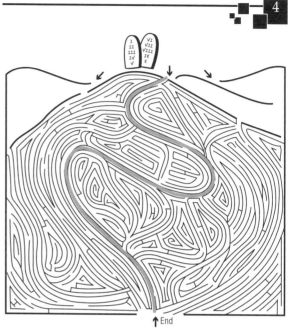

4

2

You are worthy, O Lord to receive glory and
honor and power; for You created all things, and
by Your will they exist and were created.
(Revelation 4:11)

5

3

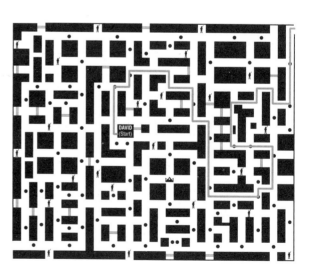

1. John	8. Lazarus
2. Absalom	9. Dinah
3. Esau	10. Hophni
4. Moses	11. Rufus
5. Benjamin	12. Gershon
6. Seth	13. Joab
7. Chilion	14. Abinadab

Household of God

6

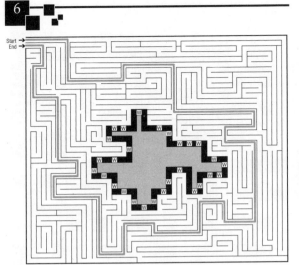

8

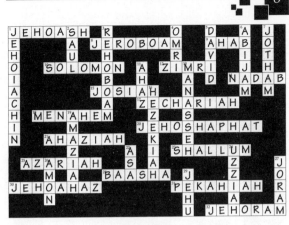

7

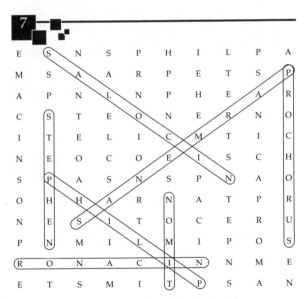

The first seven deacons are listed in Acts 6:5.

9

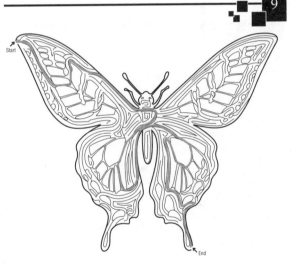

10

$$39 + 5 + 12 - 21 - 17 + 5 + 4 = 27$$

Puzzle Answers

11

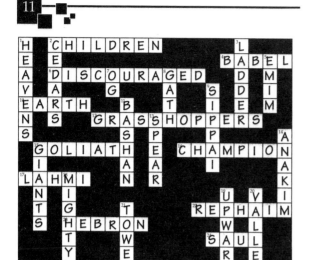

14

12

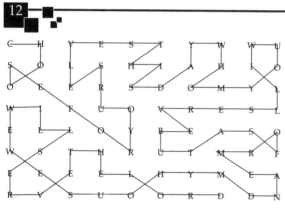

Choose for yourselves this day whom you will serve…. But as for me and my house, we will serve the LORD. (Joshua 24:15)

13

The seven churches from Revelation are Pergamos, Sardis, Ephesus, Laodicea, Thyatira, Philadelphia, and Smyrna.

1-E, 2-C, 3-G, 4-F, 5-A, 6-D, 7-B

15

Blessed are the poor in spirit, for theirs is the kingdom of heaven. (Matthew 5:3)

16

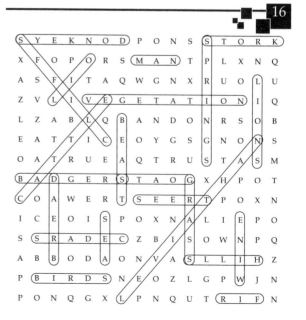

17

$$60 \times 5 + 40 \div 2 + 30 \div 20 + 5 + 20 \div 5 = 7$$

20

Blessed are those who mourn, for they shall be comforted. (Matthew 5:4)

18

21

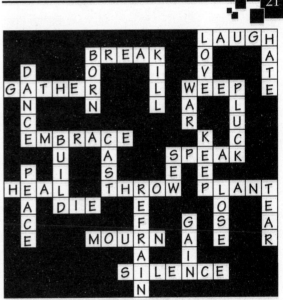

SEASON
PURPOSE

19

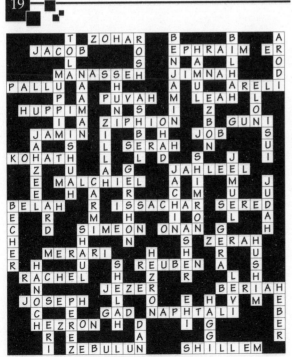

Israel's sons and daughters

PUZZLE ANSWERS

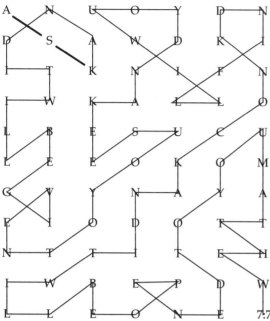

22

Ask, and it will be given to you; seek, and you will find; knock, and it will be opened to you. (Matthew 7:7)

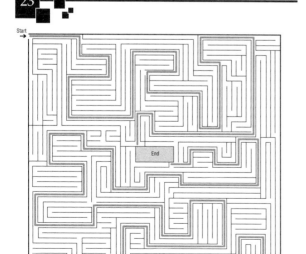

INVI**TE**
HUSBAND
WIF**E**
HONORA**B**LE
B**R**IDE
K**I**SS
WED**D**ING
F**E**AST
L**O**VE
GI**F**T
CHUR**C**H
BETROT**H**ED
BRIDEG**R**OOM
SANCT**I**FIED
GUE**S**TS
GARMEN**T**S

Come to the wedding. (Matthew 22:4)

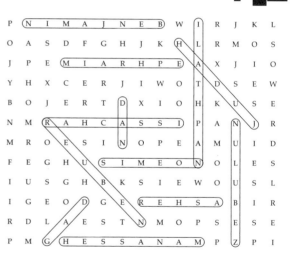

25

26

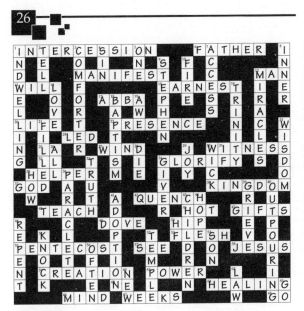

29

Bonus: MOTHER-IN-LAW

27

GABRIEL   ARCHANGEL
CHERUBIM   LUCIFER
HEAVENLY HOST SERAPHIM
MICHAEL

MESSENGER

30

$$8 \times 11 + 30 + 2 \div 4 + 40 - 10 + 21 - 52 + 2 - 6 + 10 + 5 = 40$$

31

BATTLE   LAMPS
MIDIANITES   PITCHERS
GAP   FLEECES
SHOUT

GIDEON

28

Confess your trespasses to one another, and pray for one another that you may be healed. The effective, fervent prayer of a righteous man avails much. (James 5:16, NKJ)

PUZZLE ANSWERS

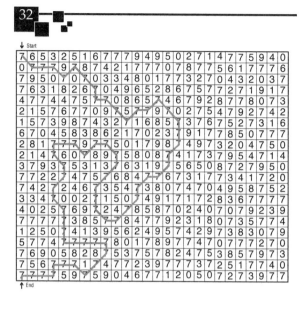

Start

End

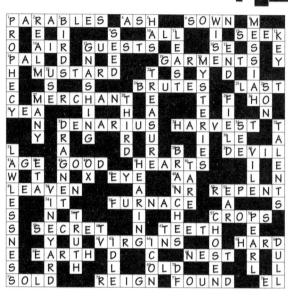

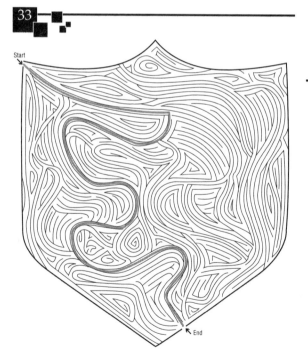

Start

End

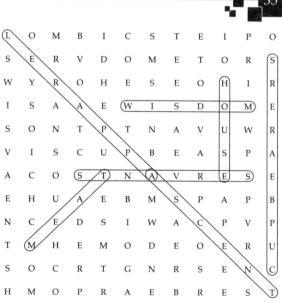

36

Behold, I stand at the door and knock. If anyone hears My voice and opens the door, I will come in to him and dine with him, and he with Me. (Revelation 3:20, NKJ)

The code is done in series of fives: 1 = A, 2 = B, 3 = C, 4 = D, 5 = E, 1 = F, 2 = G, etc.

37

Bonus: THROUGH FAITH

38

Go therefore and make disciples of all nations, baptizing them in the name of the Father and of the Son and of the Holy Spirit, teaching them to observe all things that I have commanded you; and lo, I am with you always, even to the end of the age. (Matthew 28:19-20, NKJ)

39

40

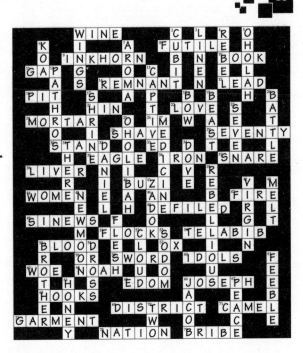

PUZZLE ANSWERS

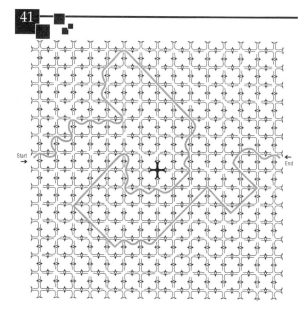

Start → ← End

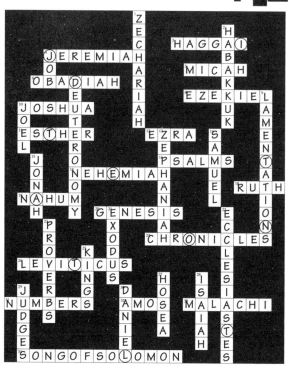

Unscrambled letters: JOT AND TITTLE

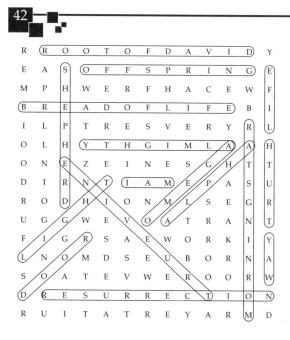

44

Unscrambled words: hand weapon, staff, vessels, ark, cross, idols, doors, cart, fire, floors, block, yokes, poles, boats, bars, canopy, bows, cherubim, manger, carved image, temple, gods, arrows, platform, table, siegeworks, musical instruments, walls, altar, offering, tabernacle, molded image, ships, boards, threshing implements, gopher, palanquin, pillars

Unscramble verse: And now abide faith, hope, love, these three; but the greatest of these is love. (1 Corinthians 13:13, NKJ)

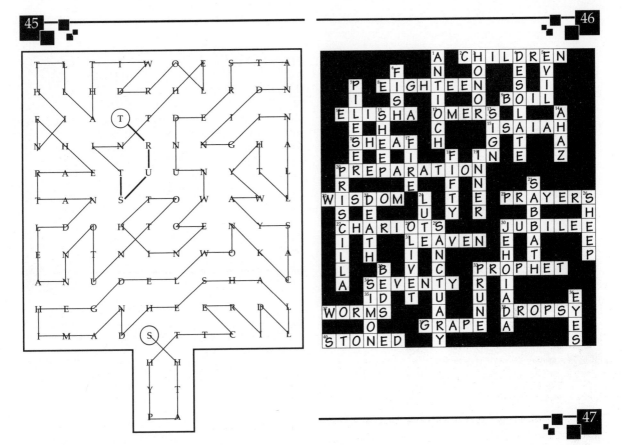

TRUST IN THE LORD WITH ALL THINE HEART; AND LEAN NOT UNTO THINE OWN UNDER-STANDING. IN ALL THY WAYS ACKNOWLEDGE HIM, AND HE SHALL DIRECT THY PATHS. (Proverbs 3:5-6)

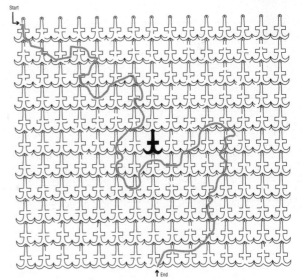

47

PUZZLE ANSWERS

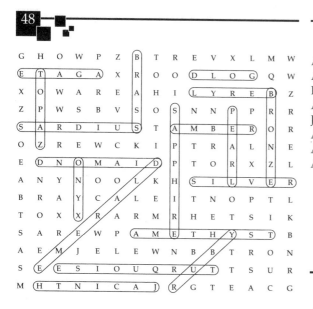

ABIRAM AND DATHAN	DOEG THE EDOMITE
ACHAN	PASHHUR
HEROD AGRIPPA I	SANBALLAT
AHAZ	REHOBOAM
JEROBOAM I	TERTULLUS
ABIHU AND NADAB	ZEDEKIAH
AMNON	ELYMAS
ATHALIAH	

TRIBULATION

For God so loved the world, that he gave his only begotten Son, that whosoever believeth in him should not perish, but have everlasting life. (John 3:16)

$$7 + 7 \times 10 \times 3 \div 6 + 14 \div 2 + 7 + 15 - 1 \div 7 - 2 = 7$$

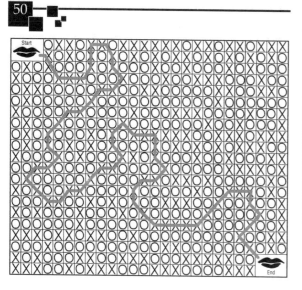

Unscrambled letters: FORGIVENESS

54

Start →
← End

56

55

TRUST
WORSHIP
STRENGTH
GLORY
DOMINION
LIFE
ENERGY
KNOWLEDGE
KINGDOM
ANSWERS
REWARD
ALLEGIANCE
HONOR
OBEDIENCE
DEVOTION
FUTURE
PRAISE
RESOURCES
MAJESTY
LOVE
CHOICE
POWER
CROWN

57

PHILISTINES   AHAB   JEZEBEL
GIDEON   AMALEKITES   JORAM
AHINOAM   ELIJAH   JEHU
ISH-BOSHETH   NABOTH   MIDIANITES

JEZREEL

Puzzle Answers

Start ↓

↑ End

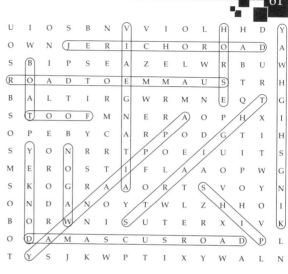

And they were all filled with the Holy Spirit and began to speak with other tongues, as the Spirit gave them utterance. (Acts 2:4, NKJ)

FREE
SPIRIT
GLORY
HEIRS
LIBERTY
LIFE
OBEDIENCE
REQUIREMENT
SONS AND DAUGHTERS
ADOPTION
PEACE
JESUS CHRIST
JUSTIFIED

RIGHTEOUSNESS

ACCUSED
OLD MAN
CARNAL
BONDAGE
FLESH
ENMITY
SIN
LAW
DEATH
GUILT
CORRUPTION
SELF-SEEKING

CONDEMNATION

The code: Take the alphabet and number from front (A) to back (Z) to middle (M, N) and repeat until all letters have a number A=1, Z=2, M=3, N=4, B=5, Y=6, L=7, O=8, C=9, X=10, K=11, P=12, and so on.

Do not be wise in your own eyes; fear the LORD and depart from evil. (Proverbs 3:7, NKJ)

64

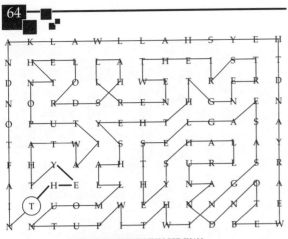

THEY THAT WAIT UPON THE LORD SHALL
RENEW THEIR STRENGTH; THEY SHALL MOUNT
UP WITH WINGS AS EAGLES; THEY SHALL RUN,
AND NOT BE WEARY; AND THEY SHALL WALK
AND NOT FAINT. (Isaiah 40:31)

65

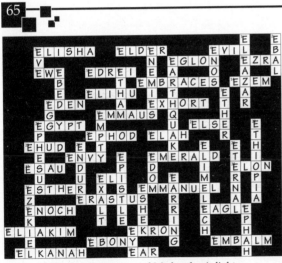

For My yoke is easy and My burden is light.
(Matthew 11:30, NKJ)

66

$$365 + 182 \times 2 - 600 + 969 - 75 +$$
$$130 \div 3 + 162 + 105 + 70 - 20 +$$
$$130 - 30 + 65 + 12 = 1000$$

67

ETHBAAL
PROPHETS
QUEEN
SIDONIAN
NABOTH
EUNUCHS

ELIJAH
DOGS
JEZREEL
VINEYARD
JEHU
AHAB

JEZEBEL

68

(crossword grid of New Testament books)

THESSALONIANS, TIMOTHY, LUKE, MARK, C, REVELATION, CORINTHIANS, HEBREWS, ROMANS, MATTHEW, JOHN, G, TITUS, JUDE, JAMES, ACTS, P, GALATIAN, EPHESIANS, PHILIP, PHILIPPIANS, PETER, EM, AN, COLOSSIANS, N

69

The code: The vowels — a, e, i, o, u — are numbers 1,
2, 3, 4, 5. The rest of the alphabet is then numbered,
beginning with 6. B=6, C=7, D=8, F=9, etc.

For unto us a Child is born, unto us a Son is given;
and the government will be upon His shoulder. And
His name will be called wonderful, Counselor,
Mighty God, everlasting Father, Prince of Peace.

PUZZLE ANSWERS

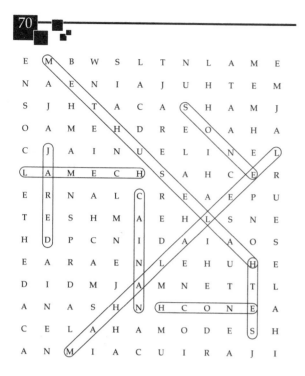

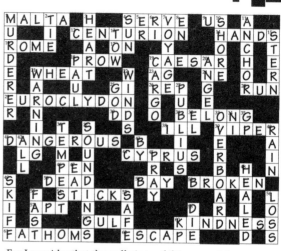

For I consider that the sufferings of this present time are not worthy to be compared with the glory which shall be revealed. (Romans 8:18, NKJ)

MOSES
LABAN
MESHA
DAVID
JAZIZ

ABEL
JACOB
LORD
JOSEPH
ABRAHAM

SHEPHERD

74

1. Do not enter the path of the wicked, and do not walk in the way of evil. (Proverbs 4:14, NKJ)

2. Honor the LORD with your possessions, and with the firstfruits of all your increase. (Proverbs 3:9, NKJ)

3. Evil pursues sinners, but to the righteous good shall be repaid. (Proverbs 13:21, NKJ)

4. A wise son makes a glad father, but a foolish son is the grief of his mother. (Proverbs 10:1, NKJ)

5. Hatred stirs up strife, but love covers all sins. (Proverbs 10:12, NKJ)

Unscrambled letters: Apples of gold

76

SORROWS
CUT OFF
STRIPES
SMITTEN
NO BEAUTY
DESPISED
BRUISED
STRICKEN
ARM
CHASTISEMENT
ROOT
WOUNDED
TENDERPLANT
REJECTED
SHEEP
GRIEF
AFFLICTED
OPPRESSED
INIQUITY

75

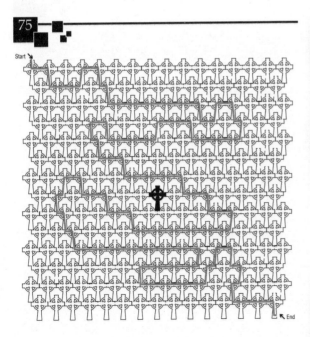

77

PUZZLE ANSWERS

78

The 13 words are the 12 disciples — plus the disciple who later replaced Judas: Philip, Simon, James, Thaddaeus, Judas, Thomas, John, James, Peter, Andrew, Matthew, Bartholomew, and Matthias.

Unscrambled letters: Praise His Name!

80

Pass through each item of offering before bringing it to Moses. Do not cross back over a path that you have already used. ◆ = Offering

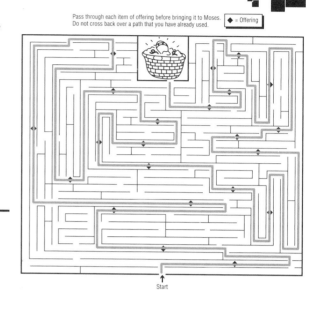

Start

79

81

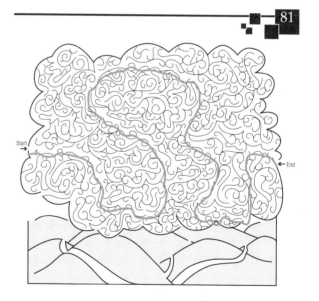

Start

End

WA**T**ER
CLOT**H**ING
F**A**ITH
DELIVERA**N**CE
KNOWLEDGE
SHELTER
FOR**G**IVENESS
INS**I**GHT
VICTORY
W**I**SDOM
FRIE**N**DSHIP
GUIDANCE
HE**A**LING
STRE**N**GTH
FOO**D**
SU**P**PLY
REWARDS
S**A**LVATION
INSP**I**RATION
PRE**S**ENCE
PROTE**C**TION

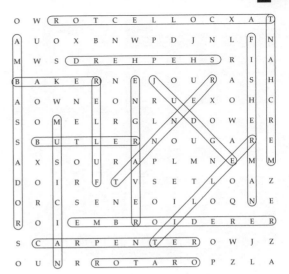

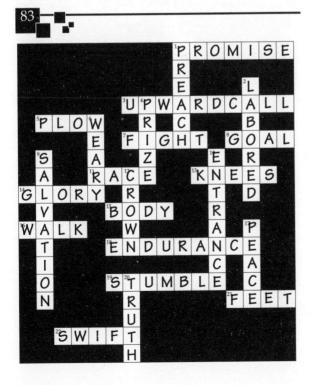

SANCTUARY
YA**H**WEH
CHILDR**E**N OF ISRAEL
AR**K** OF THE COVENANT
RAD**I**ANCE
TABER**N**ACLE
PILLA**R** OF CLOUD
HOLY PLACE
PRESENCE OF **G**OD
DWE**L**LING
MOUNT SINAI
PILLA**R** OF FIRE
MY PEOPLE

SHEKINAH GLORY

Where God dwells now:
IN YOU

PUZZLE ANSWERS

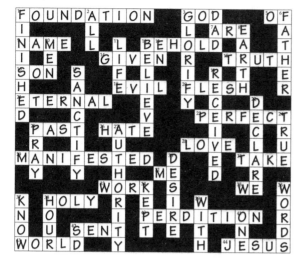

But we all, with unveiled face, beholding as in a mirror the glory of the Lord, are being transformed into the same image from glory to glory. (2 Corinthians 3:18)

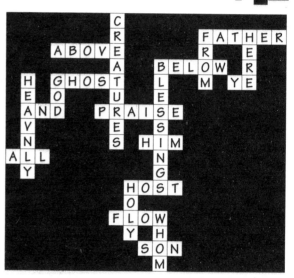